the
UNSTOPPABLE
GENERATION

ARE WE THE ONES WE
HAVE BEEN WAITING FOR?

Mona Corwin

Carpenter's Son Publishing

Published by Carpenter's Son Publishing, Franklin, Tennessee

Published in association with Larry Carpenter of Christian Book Services, LLC
www.christianbookservices.com

Cover Design by Clarissa Doll

Interior Design by Suzanne Lawing

Editing by Robert Irvin

Printed in the United States of America

978-1-940262-26-0

ENDORSEMENTS

The UnStoppable Generation is a must-read for any believer who is serious about launching a generation of warriors to fulfill the Great Commission in our lifetime. With a little over two-thousand language groups left to be reached in the world, the fulfillment is close, and this generation is breaking all the boundaries set up by man because they're passionate about the Gospel. That's a God thing! I believe we could be training the generation who will train the last generation to walk the earth, and they are the most globally-wired & globally-concerned generation in history. Mona Corwin's words ring true with provocative clarity that will energize your desire to engage this generation by making disciples who make disciples, and changing the world by starting right where you are. They're all around us, in our homes, in our churches. Let's not put them to sleep with weak religion. Let's jump in and mentor them for Kingdom IMPACT, and watch them torch the world with the Gospel!

Chris White
President, Mobilizing Students

Mona Corwin is no stranger to the value of empowering and equipping women in our generation. Her heart to see women walk confidently and purposefully in pursuit of Christ drives her life. *The UnStoppable Generation* is sure to be an invaluable resource for women seeking to live a life that glorifies God in ways that the Lord has specifically and intentionally equipped each of us.

Rebecca Benson
Associate Student Minister, Brook Hills Church
Birmingham, AL

Mona is a mother of significant influence in today's marked generation. With an incredible understanding of the Bible and the importance of women in our culture, she sees no need to sugar coat the raw truth. *The UnStoppable Generation* will be motivating and inspiring. I highly recommend it.

Alex Mohle
Dallas Baptist Graduate

As a student of the Word and of our culture, Mona's teachings bring valuable insight to women of our day. And boy do we need clarity! Let's jump in and mentor them for Kingdom IMPACT, and watch them torch the world with the Gospel!

Christy White
Board of Directors, Trek-X

This book leads you on an exciting path that will open your eyes to all that God is doing in this generation. So get ready! You're about to discover your role and purpose in this awesome generation that God has ordained for such a time as this!

Barb Leonard
Founder, Director of The Gospel to the Americas

I have benefited from Mona's wisdom for years and am so excited that now it's in print so others can profit. You will be inspired and want to be part of what God is doing among us. This work is very timely it will give clarity and vision to this unstoppable generation.

Kyle Pierson
East West Ministries

I was fresh out of college and interning at a church far from home. Mona sought me out and invited me over. She began talking about the very things that are in this book and I was intrigued, hooked, and sat for hours listening. I began to seek her out to hear more! She has passionately had this book in an "audio version" in her heart and mind for years and countless girls and women like me have benefited from hearing her speak out of the abundance of her heart. I'm thrilled that this is in print so you too can "hear" from a voice who has been there and done that on this topic!

Amy Pierson
Author/East-West Ministries

CONTENTS

ACKNOWLEDGEMENTS

Warren, my forever love, watching you is like watching Christ love the church.

My heroes, our kids, Brett, Mallory, Max, Molly, Andreza and Stacie—you make me want to be brave.

My God-given family tree: Mom Barb, Uncle Tom, CJ, Chris, Christy, Uncle Randy, and Rosie—your love and care is without measure.

Carpenter's Son Publishing: Bob, Clarissa and Suzanne for making this book so darn amazing.

Larry Carpenter—thank you for believing in authors and the gifts in us all. You are advancing publishing for a new generation.

My amazing God that makes fearlessness and grace possible. All glory is yours.

ABOUT THE AUTHOR

Mona Corwin is founder of Amazing Things Ministry, a Bible-Life Mentoring ministry that is restoring the value of womanhood and equipping the UnStoppable Generation to live open, authentic lives ablaze for Gods glory. And she is the epitome of unstoppable. Her mission and message resonates with women all over the world. Igniting hearts to come out of comfort and join the fearless. With subtle and sometimes not so subtle encourage- ment, she never allows anyone to be  a bystander in life-- Her speaking and writing inspire wom- en to enlarge their lives and be brave.

When not mentoring Mona spends her days in Texas laughing with the love of her life Warren, their 5 children, daughter-in-love and 2 grandchildren.

Her Lifeway published book on discipleship, *Table for Two* and *The Jesus Advent Tree* a family devotional are among her other works.

▶▷▶PREFACE◀◁◀

My View

We were made for such a time as this.

I'd like to call myself a grown-up, but I've never liked labels. I'm a realist, a verb girl.

I've been around awhile. The book in your hands hasn't been written by an innocent bystander who only has theories on our culture and womanhood. Instead, it's by a chick who has been on the front lines, waiting for the ones who would turn things back toward God.

I've had a front row seat to the deception and the demise of our culture. Born just after the '60s generation, I've witnessed events reaching this point: responding to the never-ending "new" ideas has become the norm. My contemporaries and I have had the task of managing the fallout of those endless "transforming" ideas . . . that have unraveled our culture, families, faith, and future.

Let's be honest, no one gets it right all the time. I don't. The deception that man has better ideas than God is as old as the Garden of Eden itself. We all sensed that something was going very wrong in our culture.

I was on the front line as the real war on women—and men for that matter—unfolded.

I watched feminism take a swing at womanhood.

I watched as I realized it was the enemy who was knocking her down.

I watched as the family became broken and bitter.

I cried at the destructive outcome: men degraded, babies destroyed, godly femininity disappeared.

I longed to know the truth of God's design for gender.

I prayed for some older women to show me the way.

I heard the wind of biblical womanhood praising and proclaiming hope.

I joyously realized I was not alone.

I repented as I laid down my bitterness at feminist theories.

I breathed in courage to fight the real enemy and exhaled praise to God.

I raised my voice, proclaimed truth, and watched as it breathed life into the women around me.

I saw hints that God was turning the hearts of a generation toward compassion for those facing injustice and to acts of courage, to be His hands and feet.

I held my breath in hope that God was breathing his life-giving love and power into His creation again.

I wondered if we were losing the battle, losing our kids, losing what God created us to be.

I settled in, waiting for the ones who would change the direction, holding my breath . . . hoping for the best but expecting . . . who knows what?

Then I saw it. I knew it when I saw it. I almost jumped from my seat (actually, I did). There it was on my computer screen; a generation was gathered together, cross-generationally, cross-racially, full of the passion for God.

Were they the ones we have been waiting for?

It was January 6, 2013 . . . 60,000 college students filled the Georgia Dome, in Atlanta. The devil must have been shaking in his boots as the sound of their worship saturated the atmosphere.

Passion 2013 was in full swing. Since 1997 the Passion movement has always been inspiring, looking like a picture of the promise of revival that so many of us pray for. But this time there was something different. Their hearts were singing . . . not songs about what God could do for them . . . But what they could do for God and *His* Glory.

On the third night of the conference, what I saw reminded me of an Old Testament verse in 1 Chronicles 12:32, a passage that describes the ancient Hebrew men of Issachar. Men who were honored by King David because they knew the word of God, understood the times they lived in, and would show Israel what to do.

1 Chronicles 12:32
"From the tribe of Issachar, there were 200 leaders of the tribe with their relatives. All these men understood the signs of the times and knew the best course for Israel to take" (NLT).

There it is, a modern-day version of the men of Issachar. In the center of the Georgia Dome was a table of fifteen wise men and women (of the '60s and '70s era, no less!) who love God and the Word. Discussing ways to impact the world and shine a light on human slavery and end slavery in our lifetime. And they were using VERBS! Action plans were already in place. Setting captives free is always on God's Top 10 list. The creativity was astounding as they laid out ideas and plans. The dome was silent as the youngest of our generation, 60,000 in all, sat on the edge of their seats listening for what they could do to be Jesus' hands and feet. The mantra was "Christ made us free for freedom." I don't know if this has ever happened before; I don't recall witnessing it in my lifetime. Friend, I was laughing and leaping for joy. They were ignited for action. Oh, and they did one other "little" thing . . . they raised more than 3.3 million dollars in just four days.

Be encouraged. This generation has arrived in its fullness. All ages, all races, all creeds, every he and every she with their vast gifts and talents all leaning forward, with one purpose—being the body of Christ and shining His light in a dark world. Whether that is overseas, stopping human trafficking, or on the career path of a stockbroker, they are embracing their slot in time for His glory.

Unlike any other generation in history, they are ready for action. Equipped with the older era imparting wisdom and the younger era igniting passion, God is about to do something marvelous in our time.

The irony is we've been looking for heroines and leaders—and now we find out it could actually be us! For if we believe that we were born for such a time as this, then we must believe that we could very well be the ones . . . that we have been waiting for.

Are you among us?

▶▷▶PROLOGUE◀◁◀

The UnStoppable Generation

Historians love to give generations names. Some generations receive honorable titles like The Greatest Generation; some are not so stately . . . the Me Generation or the X'ers. The experts relish categorizing people groups; unfortunately, this creates division and exclusivity. And whether the generation likes it or not, someone is there to give them a name.

What the historians have not yet recognized is the breed of believers hidden within today's generation. A planting of God, they are growing in numbers. Far from divided, within their ranks you will find all ages, genders, colors, and ethnic backgrounds. Breaking away from traditional definitions, they silence talk of division or gaps. In fact, they boast in diversity, proclaiming that all have worth, value, and purpose as they stand together, shoulder-to-shoulder. And just to make the historians aware, this generational line of Jesus-lovers is determined to refuse the labels of the world. As I see it, this band of Jesus-lovers has an undeniable label: the UnStoppables. They love God and His Word, and they understand the times they live in; therefore, they know what to do.

And with God's help, they do it fearlessly. Now, that is an unstoppable equation.

Different from any generation before them, there are

plenty of people who whisper, who rumor, that this generation just might include the ones we have all been praying for and waiting for. Constantly moving forward, these soul hunters are rushing into a world that needs justice and compassion. They are awake and they belong to God. The world doesn't define them, mold them, or move them. They possess a tenacity that comes from a surrendered, Spirit-empowered life.

Where did this passion come from? Could God's own heart be the answer? Could it be that decades of prayers echoing into the future have landed in our very midst? Did God hear the small-town churches pray in the '60s, '70s, and '80s? Could those prayers have piled up so high that Heaven was full, petitioning Him to send a generation that would change the world for His Glory?

Humanity crying out in moments like: October 4, 1997, when an estimated 1.5 million Christian men descended on Washington, D.C. for a Promise Keepers event called "A Sacred Assembly of Men: A Personal Day of Repentance and Prayer for Families and the Nation."

Men from all walks of life travel across the country. Chartering planes and buses just to be able to stand together—fathers with their sons, brothers, and friends. Those that gathered still testify to the spiritual gravity of that day as they all stood shoulder-to-shoulder filling the grounds between the Washington Monument and the Capitol. What pleasure God must have felt listening to a million male voices lifting prayers and praises to Heaven as they sang, "Holy, Holy, Holy."

Women have also been gathering to pray. Since 2008 the True Woman Movement has increased in numbers. They have been meeting to pray and seek God for a spiritual awakening. Calling women to embrace biblical womanhood, and to stand in the gap for their families and nation. The passion of these women, as they seek God, is an amazing sight indeed.

Is it possible? Could it be? That God has begun answering the decades of prayers during our lifetime? Some say He has already begun.

Why Does This Book Only Focus on Women?

Although this UnStoppable generation contains both genders, this book is written for the "she side" of the gender equation.

My goal is to illuminate and define God's unique design for women and how it is essential to this generation. Inspiring them to embrace that spacious design so that, along with their brothers, they can be an unstoppable influence for Jesus. It will be considered counter-cultural, but the UnStoppables have never worried about following the crowd. God's truth, and Him glorified, is their only objective. It is to this end that this book is written.

Cultural Chatter

Much of our societal culture now wants to redefine gender, and some even want to end gender altogether. In the past few years, the campaign to change God's design for man and woman has ramped up considerably as famous talk-show women have joined the conversation. The labeling and redefining have turned into arguing and name-calling. The result is more confusion.

Standing on the sidelines, Christian women are whispering, "Someone needs to do something! Someone needs to speak up and tell what God says about all this redefining."

Enter: the older women of the UnStoppable Generation. Like Joshua and Caleb of the Old Testament, they aren't afraid to tell it like it is. They are strong and courageous, eager to help the younger UnStoppables stay on track as they go through rough terrain headed for the promised land of God's plan for them. These women know the pitfalls of previous generations, and they know the culture they live in. No one would call them wimpy or weak. They have something to say, and every *she* is going to want to hear it.

When women hear about the unique "she side" of the UnStoppable Generation, they perk up, sometimes physically leaning in, curious and expecting. They have instinctively sensed that something has been missing in their understanding of gender. And they earnestly hope there is an answer.

All across our culture, from college campus to carpool lines, you can hear the voices of women crying out for someone to cut through the chaotic chatter of Hollywood and the media and cast a vision of clarity.

Today's women are bombarded with mixed messages about what it is to be a woman.

Ask the average girl on the street what femininity is and you just might hear replies like these:
- The fashionista responds: "Oh my, pink ribbons and lace, of course."
- The feminist responds: "Weak and oppressed—period."
- The chicks answer: "Ooh, baby, that's easy—push-up bras and thongs."
- And the clueless: "Um? Isn't that a new hygiene product?"

Yep, confusion abounds.

Believers, and even many nonbelievers, are frustrated with the contradicting double messages the world has flooded into the cultural conversation. Hungry for wisdom, women crave clear direction, pleading:

"We are not frustrated, angry feminists anymore; we like our men, and we don't want to be men, either."

"Will someone just be honest: What is 'she' supposed to be?"

"Is there a purpose greater than making and having babies, and what does God say, anyway?"

"Show me what it looks like. Help me with truth and propel me with courage to go against the culture if I have to."

Wanting to be brave, wanting to be fearless, they're holding their breath, waiting. Those of us who know the truth they seek have the privilege of pointing them to the answers. How can we deny breathing life into their womanhood? We must not fear, but be brave and, just like the women of Psalm 68:11, who proclaim the good news, speak bravely.

For we find *ourselves* among the ones we all have been waiting for.

What to Expect From This Book

Imagine a woman of any age picking up this book out of curiosity, wondering what an Unstoppable She looks like, and if she might be one of the ones being waited on. She's heard all the fuss about gender and is wondering what the big deal is.

She is tired of the old-line feminism banter that degrades her brothers and berates her father, husband, and the men in the world that lifted her up on her career path. She just isn't mad at men. Many of these women want clarity on how being a woman fits into her life today in her own generation. Not finding a cultural voice that speaks of another option, she usually ends up merely sighing over the confusion, wishing someone would just clearly define the thing.

Then, while flipping through the pages of this book, she is caught up in the breathtaking wonder of her design. She sees biblical femininity as relevant for today's culture and very obtainable. Finishing the last chapter, she is fully persuaded that being an UnStoppable She is not only a good thing, it is a desirable and worthy one. The outcome can be wonderful. God has infused His life-giving truth on yet another sister who, in turn, breathes life into her world, fully fragrant and feminine to the core. And so the wind of this movement continues to blow.

And as she takes her unique place alongside her brothers and sisters, she smiles, realizing that she too is now one of the ones we all have been waiting for . . . a member of the UnStoppable Generation.

PART ONE

HER GENERATION:
Finding and Defining UnStoppables

Author's Note: *This book is not a survey of where women went wrong and who's to blame. There will be no male-bashing or feminist mudslinging here, although there is plenty of mud to go around. It is, however, very important to know the history of our "she" story. Please take time to read from the list of authors in the back of this book. They have conducted impeccable research and provided documentation that provides solid truth to dispel lies.*

But if you are in a hurry, enjoy this fictional story first; it gives a quick overview of the generations of women who came before us.

DRAMA 1

Her Inheritance

"Sign here, Miss."

Taking the pen from the Fed Ex man, she scribbled her name.

"Ever feel like you're signing your life away?" he chuckled as he handed her the large, heavy box.

Ordinarily, she would have enjoyed the humorous exchange, but today wasn't an ordinary day, and this long-awaited box wasn't ordinary either.

The old wooden box, marked INHERITANCE, was heavy in her arms as she carried it to the kitchen. She had been waiting for its arrival since the day her grandmother excitedly hinted about a special inheritance box. However, on this day, there wasn't much excitement in receiving it. The arrival of the box was painful evidence that her precious Grams no longer lived in the cozy house down the street. The funeral was over, the flowers thrown out, and everything had settled down—everything except her grieving, lonely heart. Her sadness could only be lightened when she allowed her mind to wander and she imagined Grams dancing with Jesus on a heavenly street of gold.

Heavenly thoughts quickly turned to reality as her heavy, loaded arms reminded her of the box she was carrying. Setting the box on the kitchen table with a thud, she mumbled out loud: "What did Grams mean when she said it was a 'special' memory box? She acted like it was something out of a C.S. Lewis novel." A spark of joy crossed her heart as she recalled how Grams had a wonderful way of making everything special. Now that the box was in her possession, her curiosity was growing. It didn't seem very special or valuable. It was just an ordinary, old, wooden box, and frankly, it smelled bad.

The mystery was about to be over as she lifted the rickety lid. Ignoring the other objects in the box, her eyes fixed on the very top item. It was a letter, and the note had handwriting that made her eyes fill with fresh, hot tears. It read:

My sweet granddaughter,

When I was young, my grandmother gave me this box of memories, and now I lovingly pass it on to you. It is your inheritance. Dear one, we come from a long line of women who loved God but fought the curse of Eve in every generation. It is now part of your destiny to take care of their memories. These memories are treasured lessons learned by women who paid a high price for them. Costly and valuable, I pray you will heed the truths they reveal.

In this box you will find pieces of history that the world would want to hide, but we must not; they provide lessons we must never forget.

My slot in God's timeline is done, and yours has just begun. Live wise, my precious granddaughter, love God, and follow the design found in His Word . . . You were born for such a time as this. . . . And don't worry about me; all is well. I'm dancing with Jesus in my favorite pale pink satin dress.

All My Love,
Grams

The streams of tears were now mixed with laughter; she could almost hear Grams's voice trail off as she and Jesus danced away. She kissed the letter and set it by her side.

Tentatively, she approached the contents of the box. The first discovery made her giggle; she had always been told that she came from a long line of honest and humorous women. The large, ragged paper read:

From Generation to Generation HE Remains the Same . . . (We're the ones who messed up)

We hereby declare that we are a great line of women, who, over generations have been the caretakers of this box. We have each intentionally added our own objects representing lessons our generations have learned about womanhood. The memories in this box are to help you learn from our mistakes and prepare you for the deception that could come your way. You see, the curse that found its origin in the Garden of Eden follows all womanhood from generation to generation. A great price is always paid when we as "daughters of Eve" do not choose to follow the design of the God who created us. Never forget: His Word will never misguide you. It will help you heal mistakes and set your path straight again.

We now send our blessings to you, the caretaker of this box. May you be a sweet fragrance to the world, wise in knowledge of the Word, and embedded with a passion to serve the God you adore. But most of all, may you possess a faith that would render you fearless in your femininity, always bringing glory to our God.

P.S. We have shared our lessons so you can stand a little taller than your mother and grandmothers. So, when you fall and when you stumble, you too can put your object into the box next to ours. The next generation needs your honesty. The time will come when you, too, will lovingly place this inheritance box in the hands of the next generation.

Excited to discover more, she pulled out each labeled object and pondered its truth. This is what she found.

~ A **rotten apple**, whose stained label said:
"Think before you act. Childbirth really hurts."
—EVE

~ A **crown** draped in jewels
"Press into the door of the destiny God has designed for you. There is a crown on the other side."
—ESTHER

~ A **burp rag** and **reading glasses**
"You're never too old to make an impact on the world."
—SARAH, MOTHER OF ISAAC

~ A **glass box with manna** in it
"When God provides you with manna in the wilderness, eat it and be quiet."
—A WHOLE GENERATION OF WOMEN THAT DID NOT GET TO GO INTO THE PROMISED LAND.

~ A small, dusty **covered wagon**
"When traveling uncharted territory, hold on tight to your faith and your family. And instead of looking for a map, ask God for directions. He knows the way, anyway."
—WOMEN OF THE AMERICAN FRONTIER

~ A **red satin dress** with long fringes on it
"You can roar your heart away like the flappers of the roaring '20s. Little did we know we were 'fanning the flames of a rebellion.'"
—WISHING WE WEREN'T SUCH A "ROARING"-IN-THE-1920S-GENERATION

~ A **propaganda poster** of the rolled-up sleeve, with bi-cep-pumped
> *"Rosie the Riveter," entitled "We Can Do It"*
> *"Beware when the desire to build and grow and make becomes a desire to dominate."*
> —"ROSIE THE RIVETER": WOMEN OF THE 1940s

~ A perfect **strand of pearls**
> *"We wore the pearls. We fit into the cookie-cutter. But a woman wasn't meant to be beautiful on her own, but to be radiant in Christ."*
> —THE "JUNE CLEAVER" WOMEN OF THE 1950s

~ A **bra**
> *"So, you can burn your bras and find that . . . you know what? Maybe I could have used a little structure and support in my life."*
> —BURNED-OUT HIPPIES OF THE 1960s

~ A pair of **Go-Go boots**
> *"Boots are made for walking on the ground and standing for the truth, not for stomping on men."*
> —THE FEMINIST (NOT REGRETFUL) OF THE 1960s

~ A **bank account checkbook**
> *"Beware when you feel large and in charge. When you crave money and desire power, those briefcases and boardrooms can produce bossy, barren women. It may cost you more than you bargained for."*
> —THE "I WANT IT ALL" GIRLS OF THE 1970s

~ A worn-out **pair of red stiletto heels**
> *"I am woman, I am invincible; Men want me, Women envy me. I am sexy, I am desirable . . . I am pooped!"*
> —THE "I GOT IT ALL" GIRLS OF THE 1980s

~ A big, **red grading pencil**
"The Feminist Mystique was a mistake. We fought for it all, we demanded it all, and we got it all. Now we are running it all, more exhausted and discontent than ever. It's never enough! Anyone know how to rewind this thing?"
—THE FEMINIST OF THE MILLENIUM

She had reached the end of the treasures in the box when she noticed one more. It was wrapped. She had enjoyed the other objects and, with anticipation, she unwrapped the last one. Her smile was bigger than ever as she gazed at the leather Bible amidst the wrapping. She knew this Bible well, for it belonged to Grams. It too had a label on it.

"The greatest good for all womanhood is to be transformed into the likeness of Christ and reflect Him to a dying world, in a way that only a woman can. Don't be wimpy women, be fearless in your femininity so that all will see the glory of God. You were made to be unstoppable."
–The True Woman-Generation

Holding the Bible close to her heart, she exclaimed: "Grams, you are that woman! Hmmmm . . . What will I leave in the box?" She instinctively knew, and ran to her room to retrieve her contribution for the box.

It was a small, pink jewelry box that, when opened, revealed a perfect, tiny ballerina that danced and turned to music. In glitter on the lid were the words:

I'm a Diva Princess and The World Revolves Around ME.

She laughed, but was also saddened by the truth those words revealed. She had become a self-absorbed, perfect, all-about-me diva. Head and finger snaps accessorized the way she treated others, including men.

Unfortunately, she knew she wasn't alone. Many in her generation looked the same. "Ugh!" she sighed, talking to herself softly. "We have spent so much time staring at ourselves that we forgot what we look like. Distracted by our beautiful reflections, we forgot what we were here to do. Our generation must be different. Surely there are others who want something more."

I'll have to label this later. Surely there will be a better name than "all about me" for a generation that has been given so much, she thought as she placed her unlabeled contribution into the old wooden box, closing the rickety lid.

Walking away from it, a new sense of resolve hit her soul. What truths she had discovered. What pitfalls she would now be alert to. A new hunger for truth and wisdom overcame her. The generations of women who came before her had done their part.

All of them seemed to want wisdom. Some believed lies, but some embraced truth when God revealed it, impacting their generations for good. Every generation is given their chance to live and choose the legacy they leave. Grams had lived well in her slot in God's timeline. And now, armed with advice from previous generations and the Word of God, she resolved to find God's original design for womanhood in her own generation. She was now fully confident that the God who called her to this journey would supply the answers she needed. She giggled a quiet giggle. Could she be what Grams had described? Could she be "unstoppable"?

Excitement and boldness overcame her as she prepared to face the rest of what started out as an ordinary day. It was then that a peace and joy flooded her that only God could provide, and she realized that nothing about her life would ever be ordinary again.

She felt as if she was walking straight into her destiny. With her grandmother's Bible held close to her heart, she could almost feel the flame of passion inside her. She had been given a great heritage to pass on. Surely it would be counter-cultural, but that mattered not; she knew she was called for such a time as this. Her only desire now was to allow the imprint of God, which was in her, to impact the world around her. Not for power, money, or self, but only for *His glory*. And then, joyfully, placing the legacy of that inheritance, still well intact, to her daughters.

She longed to fan the flame of biblical femininity like no other generation before her. Confident that, with God's help, she would be a sweet fragrance within the generation in which He had placed her. To do this, she would need to have a femininity that was full to the core and faith in her God, and she would need to walk fearlessly in her world. Yes, Grams just might have been right naming her . . . UnStoppable.

ONE

▶ ▶ ▶ ▶ ▶ ▶ ▶ ▶

Awakening a Generation

Remnant: *a trace; vestige: remnants of former greatness*

Revival: *a new presentation of an old play or similar vehicle*

Reveal: *to lay open to view; display.*

WAKE UP!

The clock is still ticking. And time is moving on. People are born, live, and die in their time slots of history. Generations come and go. God alone knows the purpose of each generation as he moves the clock closer and closer to the time He deems time will be no more. He decides. It's His story and He, as Creator, is the author of it all. Playing on words, without being cheesy, History is *His story*. It's all about Him and His Glory.

Time is God's idea. He created it, and He is not bound by it. Eternally present, He did not, and does not, require time. However, His creation, mankind, does. The sin that man chose in the Garden of Eden brought both death and a great need for time into our life.

And the clock started ticking.

In time, God took care of the eternal death, the separation-from-Him-forever, when he sent His son, Jesus, to pay the penalty of sin by dying on the cross at Calvary. Salvation is now available to all who would receive it. However, God predetermined to leave time in place for his purposes, until the fullness of time is completed.

> *He calls our generation to take center stage.*

Even with all this wonder, man's Eden-thinking still remains. Convinced it's all about us, we believe that God created everything for our pleasure. We live our own individual timeslots as if we are the main character in history's unfolding story. Confident that God will be pleased as we invite Him to play a supporting role in the life we are creating. How foolish we are.

Funny thing about God: He totally gets us. He loved Adam and Eve in their rebellion and He loves us in ours. Miraculously, He still desires to include us in His story. The God of all creation invites us to be a part of the long line of generational believers who have already lived out God's script for their lives. Now, it is up to us to choose whether to accept His plan as He calls our generation to take center stage.

Hearing The Call?

Many will hear Him. Not everyone answers God's call. Yet among generation after generation, there is always a remnant of people that God finds to be His light in the world. All mankind was made in the image of God, but not all bear His name. Just as a newborn child takes the name of their father, so do those who are born again in

Christ bear His name. But there is a problem. God is calling, but most of what He is hearing is . . . ZZZZZZZ. The sound of slumber is coming from God's people.

Many are hitting the snooze button for their stage-call, spiritually sleepwalking in a world that denies God.

A revival of epic proportions will be needed to awaken an entire generation. Asleep in apathy and comfortable, self-focused lives, it is going to take a special breed to accomplish such a task. These people may look ordinary. But like the men and women of Acts, ordinary looks ordinary until God's power arises. Then God accomplishes the extraordinary. The results will be UnStoppable.

A revival may come, but it cannot and will not unless there is an awakening first. You may have already awoken from your slumber and, with eyes wide open, you are now realizing that you are a part of this quiet awakening of a generation. If so, wake a brother or sister or two. Then the two of you wake another one. For this awakening won't be quiet for long.

Jim Hylton put the process into words, and perfectly so.

> *"My conclusion is that the awaited awakening is a far bigger agenda than simply awaking the church to what the church was engaged in before sleep came. Our vision is too small and our agendas too limited. We are to awaken to something bigger than revival and self-consciousness. Our awakening to Christ the King, and the Kingdom, His life in action is God's goal."*[1]

But, God is able. He is the architect of great revivals. His method: Great revivals of history only come from great awakenings of His children.

Seems simple enough.

Lawrence Tribble, famous for his contribution to the Great Awaking of his time, knew this was true when, in the 1770s, he penned the poem "Awaken." Longing for another awakening, the band LeeLand put music to Tribble's poem. It can be found on their 2011 Grammy-nominated CD "The Great Awakening." [2]

Awaken
One Man awake,
Awakens another.
The second awakens
His next-door brother
The three awake can rouse a town
By turning
The whole place
Upside down.
The many awake
Can make such a fuss
It finally awakens
The rest of us,
One man up,
With dawn in his eyes,
Surely then,
Multiplies

Awakening to the Light

The reviving that is taking place has not been reported by electronic media or in the newspapers. Hidden, it takes place in the inner life of a believer. Revival is not for a building or a denomination. It is for God's people, the ones that bear His name and carry His light. And that's exactly where He starts. It is not forced or manmade; God is the producer. He shines His light into the sleeping soul of a believer. The light of true love ignites a flame. That flame, in their hearts, is burning up unbelief, sin, shame, and guilt. What's left in those hearts is faith, salvation, righteousness, freedom, and grace. The flame continues to burn with the presence of the Holy Spirit. The joy that settles in the heart is effervescent; you can see it on faces bubbling up to the surface of these lives. Now that is glorious! Christ in them—the hope of His glory shown outside of them. A.W. Tozer calls these believers "the fellowship of the burning heart."[3] Do you perceive it?

Many in this generation are experiencing this stirring, producing a deep excitement within their ranks. As they gather, you can sense they have something in common. Listen as they converse, and you will also feel the expectancy. God is reviving them and He is in their midst. They can't help but share what they are experiencing. As they tell their story, the ones who listen are drawn to God's truth and an awakening of *their* heart begins a revival within them. And then they go and tell some more.

It's like they are on a mission to tell others. Interestingly, that is exactly what God designed us as believers to do. Go out and tell. And what a story we have to tell! Proclaiming the wonders of God working in us and in our generation. Do you know it?

Reviving What?

Let's get real. We, as mere humans, do not have the power to produce a Christ-kind of revival in our institutions and religions. Laughingly, we act as if Christ is the one that needs to be revived. That He is the one sleeping. Christ doesn't need to be revived; He wants to be revealed. Revealed through a life that is ready to go and imprint the world with His glory.

The Church?

The church is not the Kingdom. Jesus spoke of "the Kingdom" 80 times and of the church 2 times. He brought the Kingdom with him when He came to earth. He left it for the body of Christ—His church and His people—to walk in.

God is not reviving a building or a denomination. He is reviving His body, His bride, the church of His original design. It's about people, not programs.[4]

To be clear, the church in America today does not look like the original church of Acts in the Bible. There are problems in organized religion in all denominations. And it doesn't matter the size or where the church building is located. She has been taking a lot of hits from the enemy lately. These have produced strife and slander among the churches. It must hurt God's heart to see such fighting among the ones he loves so dearly. Truth is, Jesus died for the church as a whole body. We are one in Him. Man created the multitude of denominations and programs.

Many have been praying for a generation that will unite God's people and spread the Gospel in every nook and cranny of this whole world. Ones who will reveal the Kingdom that Christ brought with Him. Could it be that in this generation, the members of the fellowship of the burning heart are the ones that we all have been waiting for? What an extraordinary privilege to be a vessel, molded and equipped, to proclaim His Kingdom to the world.

"God's story is being written, not thousands of years ago, but today. The pages and chapters of our generation have room for one more hero. You. You will write a chapter whether you like it or not."
—Claude Hickman[5]

God is breathing revival into his children. They have awakened from their apathy and slumber with a hunger and a thirst for God, His Word, and His people. Their passion is growing, their faith emboldens. They just aren't satisfied doing the same old churchy things anymore. No longer boasting that their lives are glorified when God is in them. They rejoice that God is the one receiving glory through the lives they willingly have given to Him.

Created to bear His name, His light, for His glory and His kingdom. Toby Mac wrote a song that embodies the truths of this generation; coincidently, it is called "Unstoppable." Check out a sample of the lyrics, then enjoy listening to the entire song online; it will have your heart beating.

"Unstoppable" by Toby Mac[2b]
We make our moves in mysterious ways
We'd rather burn up, than stick to the shade
Not of this world so we live on the run
We keep our eyes set on what is to come
We are, we are, we are unstoppable
We are, we are, for the impossible.
We are, we are, we are the kingdom come
That's who we are, that's who we are.

This new breed of light-bearers . . . impatient to impact the world, they know that for something to shine, it first has to be lit. So they are heading out into unknown territory, striking a match, and igniting every corner they can find.

The UnStoppable Generation. Are you among them?

TWO

The Good News about the Bad News

The legacy story of the UnStoppable Generation is not fully written. No one but God knows what they will or won't accomplish. There are many questions to be answered and directions to be taken. One thing is for sure—he has called them for such a time as this. Clearly they have a purpose in this timeslot on the timeline of eternity. And there is an excitement in their midst.

They are the largest generation ever produced in America. And they have been born into an era full of confusion and change. Confusion is everywhere; "redefining" is taking place across the board—from the purpose of government, to families, to marriages, and even to the church.

The UnStoppables are very acquainted with the breakdown of the walls of all these institutions. Clearly they have watched the family implode and marriages break up (50 percent of all Christian marriages end in divorce).

Politicians lie and cheat, leaving the economy in shambles, with a rising unemployment rate.

You would think that the struggling everyman would find peace and hope in their churches, yet that is not what they are finding there, either.

Where They Aren't

The research engines like the Barna Group and Gallup Poll have recently reported statistics that show the numbers of church involvement in America as declining. And the 18-to-30 age group count among us is the highest of those absent from church.[6]

As early as 2005, the Barna Group was already tracking this trend on believers leaving the church:

> *"There is a large and rapidly growing population of Christ-followers who are truly wanting to be like the church we read about in the book of Acts. We began tracking their spiritual activity and found that it is much more robust and significant than we ever imagined—and, frankly, more defensible than what emerges from the average Christian church. But, because the Revolution is neither organized nor designed to create an institutional presence, it typically goes undetected."[7]*

Clearly, there is discontentment within all age groups. Are the UnStoppables among these statistics? Yes, many have left the doors of the church.

There may be many reasons for this exit. Some of the most recent research reveals that a shocking 57 percent of 18-to-29-year-olds who claim to be Christians say they are less active in church today compared to when they were 15. And that's just one age group.[8] Their parents and mentors who agree, have also left. Many UnStoppables of all ages report that the tired approach of "doing church" is one of the culprits for their exit.

The Separatist

Separatists are people who "do church" for the *growth* of the church. They serve in the church to provide for the church and the needs of the members. There is plenty to do in the whirlwind of activity. Lots of new programs, activities, and building campaigns fill their calendars. A separatist church or a separatist Christian can be found in a small country church or a mega one. The size of the church is not an indicator of the believer's heart. Honorably, many focus on bringing the unsaved to faith in Jesus. However, their methods within the church are draining the church's influence and presence in the culture. They are pulling people away from their environments, where they could be a witness, into the church walls to volunteer for yet one more program that fills the needs of the church.

Members are encouraged to bring more people to church. There, everyone is entertained in a hip and relevant way, evangelizing as many as possible, to have more people that will, in turn, go get more people to come to church. The church is the machine that drives it all. UnStoppables see the separatist as self-focused on the inner-church community instead of reaching out to the world that is dying outside its walls.

Blenders

Then there are the blenders. People who go to church but who don't want to be seen as "those crazy Christians." So they try to blend their Christianity quietly into society. Still doing good things to help others, these blenders will say they want to show the world Jesus. They just want to be quiet when they do this. The focus is self-preservation and maintaining the pet sins they love more than God.

Afraid of being ostracized by the culture, they long to fit in—and so they do. Truth be told, their everyday lives look more like they follow the beliefs of an unbeliever than living out a belief system as a follower of Christ.

Leaving the Doors

Just as the Old Testament hero Nehemiah wept as he saw the destruction and lack of care for the temple walls, the UnStoppables are also sad for the breakdown of the church in their generation. They find themselves witnessing the trouble but having no idea how to fix it. Many churches are making course-corrections. Sadly, many are not. The UnStoppables have a love for the body of Christ and know that community is part of the original design. So, they are staying as long as they can to help facilitate change. They want to experience the Jesus that they have given their lives to in a very real way. But when they go to church they are experiencing less and less of what they think Christianity is supposed to be. Sadly, many leave the church and head out to find another way.

How many are there out there? No one knows for sure because they can't be counted. They no longer reside in the places where people count people. They have exited those doors, many never to return. A sad statement to make, yet . . . the truth is truth.

But take heart and be confident in this fact: while they have left the church, they have not left Jesus. Just like Nehemiah, who took "Just Do It" to a whole new level, could they unknowingly be about to restore the church of Jesus Christ to its original design and intent? Could the UnStoppables be the restorers we have been waiting for?

Restorers

Many UnStoppables I have spoken with believe restoring is one of the most prominent attributes of an UnStoppable. This is the very good news about the bad news. Feeling disconnected from the separatists and the blenders, they instinctively know something is missing. They don't want to disconnect from the world around them or blend into it either. Knowing the Bible does not proclaim hiding in the church or hiding within the culture, they are looking for another way to live out the passion of their faith.

And they are finding it.

As they search to restore the heart of the church to its core principles as they see them, the world is taking notice of this new breed of believers. Some say they are abandoning their faith, but whole-heartedly, they would disagree. They believe they are making changes to preserve their faith. Good and bad reviews abound as those called UnStoppables are drawing attention to themselves. Undeniably, they have a tenacity and zeal that draws people to their unique style and way of living. It's not new to planet earth, this lifestyle they are choosing. Reminiscent of the early church of Acts, their faith is ingrained into every section of their lives.

Restoring is one of the most prominent attributes of an UnStoppable.

Though they excel in their careers, gifts, and talents, this generation is all about relationships and community. They have a wonderful humility that embraces excellence without putting down the mediocre. Mistake-makers are also mercy-givers. They proclaim solid biblical truths in their lifestyles without judging others who live differently. They are generous with their time, money, and gifts. They hold to the precept that the most valuable thing on earth isn't fame or wealth, but people who are made in the image of God.

Quiet? Nope, this breed is not quiet. And they are being heard, speaking up, and showing up as the church to the lonely and hurting. Injustice sets them into action and they are not deterred by the size of the battle. Unlike other generations, they actually believe they can win. God has infused them with an unstoppable mentality that is a fresh breeze in Christendom.

And this leaves many wondering if they are the long-awaited ones who are destined to awaken the church and restore her to her designed beauty.

THREE

A Glimpse at the Path Ahead

The UnStoppable Generation looks a lot like the gang that stood at the Jordan River with Joshua and Caleb. They, like their Old Testament counterparts, are looking for a place to land. They are excited to go into the promised land that was just a water's-edge away, yet feeling not-so-equipped. Not to worry—God always provides fresh supplies in new territory. Go ahead and get wet.

Fresh Plans

Getting on the wrong path is a place an UnStoppable has been before. Their natural desire to help and be like Christ has them sometimes rushing too quickly into plans that might be for someone else. Even good plans, done in the flesh without God's provision, fizzle out.

"The reason why even Christians are still searching

*for purpose is that they try to take their new full-col-
ored puzzle pieces and cram it back into their old
black and white picture."* — Claude Hickman[9]

They are frustrated with trying to accomplish their
dreams and plans on their own. Their cry needs to be:
"God, make us ready! Ready to die to our ideas and embrace the path you have for us." For the fresh plans God
has for this new breed will be colorful indeed. God's Word
promises those plans and He also promises to supply for
them if we seek Him with all of our hearts.

Jeremiah 29:11 promises that He has plans.

> *"For I know the plans I have for you," declares the
> LORD, "plans to prosper you and not to harm you,
> plans to give you hope and a future"* (NIV).

And Ephesians 3:20 confirms how He will accomplish
them.

> *"Now to him who is able to do immeasurably more
> than all we ask or imagine, according to his power
> that is at work within us"* (NIV).

We get to walk in all of these promises with Him when
we die to ourselves and live out Jeremiah 29:12 and 13.
UnStoppable: look this passage up in your Bible!

Fresh People for Prayer

Breathing fresh life into His people is a specialty of God.
Ezekiel 37 is one of those occasions. God showed Ezekiel
a vision of a valley full of dried-up bones. He told Ezekiel
to speak to the dead dry bones, and tell them God was
going to breath life into them again and that they would
be a great army. Ezekiel did, and God did. Although it
was a vision for the Israelites, God can and does em-

power generations throughout time to bring revival to his people. And just as the Spirit breathed life into those dry bones of old, he is breathing life into the dry places of our world today.

Only this time it won't be a vision.

Pete Greig described a modern-day "dry bones moment" in *Red Moon Rising*. This is a book that may be sitting, marked and wrinkly, on many UnStoppables' bedside tables. In 1999, on the very first night of the 24/7 Prayer Movement, Pete wrote the following poem on the wall. Little did he know that he was describing a new breed of believers that would show up worldwide.

The Vision

The vision is JESUS: obsessively, dangerously, undeniably Jesus.

The vision is an army of young people.

You see bones? I see an army.

And they are FREE from materialism -

They laugh at 9-5 little prisons.

They could eat caviar on Monday and crusts on Tuesday. They wouldn't even notice.

It gave up the game of minimum integrity long ago to reach for the stars.

It scorns the good and strains for the best.

It is dangerously pure.

Such heroes are as radical on Monday morning as Sunday night.

They don't need fame from names.

And the army is discipl(in)ed — young people who beat their bodies into submission.

The advertisers cannot mold them.

Hollywood cannot hold them.

That's the Vision

— Pete Greig[10]

The 24/7 Prayer Movement is one of those fresh-wind

moments on the timeline of God. It is part of an "acciden-
tal" international prayer movement that began in September 1999, when a bunch of young people in England
got the crazy idea of trying to pray nonstop for a month.
Their idea wasn't so crazy after all. 24/7 movement is still
praying and has gone viral on the Internet.

Pete Greig recalls:

> Before, The Vision was being printed in magazines,
> remixed by DJs in New York and Sweden and even
> choreographed in Spain! In August 2001 The Vision
> was published in a magazine called "The Way"
> which circulates a staggering 100,000 underground
> churches in China. The very same week the words
> were quoted by 10,000s of American young peo-
> ple at an event called "The Call" in Washington DC.
> Somehow the words scrawled on a Prayer Room
> wall had taken on a life of their own. The Vision had
> become a personal mission statement for many—a
> generational call to arms. The Vision made us real-
> ize that God was doing something with our prayers,
> something immeasurably bigger than we could
> "ask or hope or imagine." Perhaps it's another indi-
> cation that the Spirit really is moving across the na-
> tions, uniting the generation with one dream, one
> passion, and one Commander in Chief.[11]

It is this kind of power that is fueling this awakening produced by God. The power of prayer is at the core. It will
be instrumental in what is accomplished. Restoration will
only come when prayer is ignited in the midst of God's
people. From the beginning of time, prayer has always
been on God's mind. For it is how He communes with His
children.

The simple fact that UnStoppables are awake and moving is evidence that the prayer echoes from past believers have transcended time and geography. Could the
prayers from generations past now be answers provided

in movements like 24/7 prayer, leaving the UnStoppables landing in our midst?

Fresh Avenues

The UnStoppable mindset is globally wired from living in the technology explosion that has put smart-phones and the Internet at their fingertips. The world just doesn't seem as big as it once did. With full access to what is going on in the world, many are now globally concerned. The heart of God that beats in them aches as the horrors of human injustice and pain continue day after day.

Many are torn between the American dream and the Kingdom dream. How can they develop their God-given talents and gifts in college and still reach the nations with the Gospel? How can they still raise families comfortably while people in some nations are in chains through human trafficking? Putting their passions on the back burner while doing the climb up the American ladder? God says . . . throw it all in the pot on the front burner and let's start feeding people.

This is one of those areas where some redefining of institutions and social outreach can benefit the Kingdom of God.

This is one of those areas where some redefining of institutions and social outreach can benefit the Kingdom of God. The tension between the American dream and the Kingdom dream has brought about some promising avenues that didn't exist before the Internet. Be sure of this: As God places a passion on a heart for a particular issue, be looking, for

He already has a plan and a path to accomplish it. He is very creative in how He gets things done. For instance, college students who have fallen in love for missions, yet want to get their degree, have an amazing new avenue called Trek-X.

Trek-X is an elite four-year missionary training journey designed to train, disciple, and launch students to the nations with the Gospel while allowing them to complete their education at the same time. Trek-X provides a unique platform for this motivated generation. (You can find them at www.mobilizingstudents.com .)[12]

Chris White, founder of Trek-X, speaks boldly about changing our expectations from the way things have always been and allowing for God to interrupt our plans. He says:

> *"I long for a day when we as Christian parents live for things that matter ten million years from now and not just spend our energies chasing the dollar to retirement, which isn't a biblical concept anyway. When we do that, our kids will grow up in a faith-filled home that launches them to torch the world with the Gospel in ways we never dreamed. We will write books on how this generation of fearless warriors completed the Great Commission of Christ in their lifetime."[13]*

Creative avenues like this will be needed for these amazing world-changers who want to tell the world about Jesus. And remember, the path is not the destination; it is the pipeline to the call of God to join Him in the journey.

Fresh Perspectives

They have been wandering for quite awhile, this generation. Looking for a place to land. It might be said that their theme song should be the U2 rock classic, as sung by Bono: "I Still Haven't Found What I'm Looking For." UnStoppables are looking for a new perspective, a new way to accomplish the vision and passion that is in their lives. And they don't want to do it alone. New ways to connect together as a church community, and to live out the Great Commission, are popping up all over.

Church of the City, in Nashville, is one of those churches. Through neighborhood churches, small groups, and city-wide gatherings, these believers are on mission to bring the love of Christ, wrapped in servanthood, to one of the fastest-growing cities in the nation. Missional groups within each neighborhood church cultivate partnerships with schools and social services to redeem and renew their own neighborhoods. The mode is a highly relational and deeply interdependent Kingdom-focused vision for the church.[14]

The new generation of believers has thrown out the idea that sharing the Gospel and teaching the Word is for the career pastors and missionaries in far-off lands. They insist that this kind of definition excuses people from being on a mission everyday in their workplaces. They proclaim that being a believer in Christ is your first mission in life; your call or gifting should be secondary.

So, if a believer is a dentist, they are a believer—on mission—as a dentist.

Fresh Courage to Cross Over

We are reminded again of Joshua and the wilderness generation. God told Joshua to be "strong and courageous" more than a few times. Telling someone to be brave is easy, but giving him or her the tools to do it is priceless. God gave Joshua the Word of God and told him to meditate on it and do what it said and that would make his way prosper. God's Word is still in the business of cre-

> *God's Word is still in the business of creating fearless men and women. The UnStoppable Generation will need to be diligent about knowing how to read and learn from the Word of God.*

ating fearless men and women. The UnStoppable Generation will need to be diligent about knowing how to read and learn from the Word of God. Tragically, there has been a serious lapse of teaching in how to study the Bible and glean from it. But if they are going to be UnStoppable, there is no other source for faith or courage, period.

Fresh Spreading Out

So where are the UnStoppables heading? In a word . . . out.

Heading out into the world that has no parameters. They will not be bound to the fences of the world or the walls of any church. Mobilized intergenerationally, energized biblically. Motivated by the love of God. They bear His name and live for His glory to be seen. Growing organically, their numbers are multiplying. Some call it a grassroots movement. But those who have been in the midst of the UnStoppables will tell you it's more like a grass fire. And it will spread as they connect and pursue Jesus and His Word. This is just the beginning of their journey to their legacy.

Wonder Where They Are?

They are in every field, city, and country of our world. It makes sense to them that if God said to go to the ends of the earth, that would mean every place in between. Start looking; you might even be living next to one!

Every so often you might get a glimpse of them gathering. The Passion movement is one of those gatherings. Starting in 1997, with two thousand people, the "passion" for a new way to be a Christian conference has grown to 60,000 attendees in 2013. Participants are putting their money where their mouth is, paying up to $300 for a four-day conference ticket. They filled the Georgia Dome with praises and received inspiring lectures on the holiness of God.[15] Not your average concert night! And speaking of concerts, they sell those out too. According to the *Christian Post*, Hillsong United, a popular Australian band, swept through the U.S. in 2013, on a twelve-city tour, where they played to more than 80,000 fans in only three weeks.[16]

Fresh Worship

Worship is one of their defining marks. There is no doubt that there is something different about them when you see them worship.

And it pleases the heart of God. Many times in the Bible, God would gather His people together and prepare them for a journey or battle. Often, as they obediently headed out, worshippers would lead the way singing His praises. The people, surrendered to God, would follow behind, faith in their hearts and worship on their lips. For they knew, in Him, the victory was theirs.

Many believe that worship will be at the forefront of this present movement of God. We are entering a time of great chaos and spiritual warfare. It could well be that in the days ahead, worship will bring everyone the greatest power and peace. For within the praises of His people, God can always be found.

Take note: It has been said that these sold-out believers worship with an abandonment that has never been seen before on this earth. The sight is nothing short of phenomenal. Surely, God is in their midst. As they sing with the same beat, they are connecting as one heart and offering praises to the one true God, who takes pleasure in their worship.

Listen. Can you hear them?

FOUR

Erasers and Paintbrushes

As believers, God's grace forgives all our sins and they don't count in Heaven anymore. And because he loves us so much, he has also given us erasers and paintbrushes for here on earth. Specially designed to erase our earthly, fleshly actions and paint new ones that reflect the beauty of Christ. It is a wonderful gift. –M.C.

What happens when the all-about-me generation gets saved and turns into all-about-Him? Grace, forgiveness, and mercy show up, that's what. Faith rises as they move onto the world's canvas and start creating a grace space. For, in this era of UnStoppable, determination has a face, grace has a place, and heroes have erasers and paintbrushes.

UnStoppables are well known for their ability to pull out their God-given erasers and lend a hand to others living in past sin and deception. Erasing "red pencil" mistakes and locating hurts can be a bit of a process, but they aren't rushed. God's salvation already removed the failing grade; it's just the residue of shame and guilt that makes this eraser necessary. Plus, they know that with God's continuing flow of grace, even the toughest of stains go away.

No longer moved by potential punishment from God, they are in awe of the love He has for them. Pure love that is not based on performance. That love persuades them

Once found, the old "give me, give me" gang becomes the "give you" victors that paint a new picture of freedom for themselves and others.

to trust that His promise will be life-giving to them as well as others. Hungry for truth, they search to renew their minds in the Bible. Once found, the old "give me, give me" gang becomes the "give you" victors that paint a new picture of freedom for themselves and others.

Their influence is undeniably based in the true restoration of their own lives. Not hiding their past sin or experiences in the shadows, they happily share how God healed the wounds of mistakes and hurts. They will show you the scars on their hearts and sometimes even their bodies that still exist. Unafraid, they valiantly expose those scars, allowing them to be a testimony to the glorious work God has done in their lives. For them, showing scars isn't scary; it's exciting. Jesus healed them and gave them a new life in Him. And quite frankly, life in the shadows just doesn't fit them anymore—God's grace erased the shame and painted a new path. They now live a wholehearted life and things have been colorful ever since.

Erasers and Paintbrushes
Old ways transformed into new-inspired days;
The look of relevance changed into a face of
restoration.
Followers of trends are now trail makers.
Finger pointers become problem solvers.
Professions become callings.
Flip-flopping lives become days full of purpose.
Culture of consuming becomes a culture of serv-
ing.
Shadows of pain gone; only colorful grace scares
remain.
Erasing earthly dark sin, painting hearts with Christ
within.
— M.C.

And on it goes as the paintbrushes of God's design keep stroking the canvass of their souls; sharing grace and giving mercy. The Gospel and the love of God proclaimed. Now, that is very good news.

"I would have despaired if I had not believed that
I would see the goodness of the Lord in the Land of
the Living" (Psalm 27:13, NASB).

When faced with social injustice they tend to be proactive rather than reactive. Outrage at the social injustice they see across the world motivates them to find solutions for seeking and finding the afflicted. Disheartened that people made in the image of God that He values so highly, would be so violently abused, propels them to action. And although they are passionate about injustice, they are optimistic in nature, believing that with God anything is possible. One example is The End It Movement, whose high goal is to end human slavery and sex trafficking in our lifetime.

Continually moving forward in the plan of God, coloring outside the lines is one of their specialties. For they truly believe in their erasers and paintbrushes, given by God. UnStoppables have a knack for seeing the way things ought to be or could be. Their "why not?" attitude gives life to the restoration. For they know that Jesus opens doors that no man can shut.

Gabe Lyons, prominent researcher says this about the next Christians.

> *I've seen this restoration way of thinking and living define a new generation of Christians in our world. They simply can't help themselves; they are intoxicated with the idea that God's love extends to all people. They believe this kind of love is expressed best in tangible, physical acts of goodness. They show up. In fact, showing up is their defining practice.*[17]

Simple Christianity

Where does all this painting take place? In community—grace-painted community. It's simply the way Christ did church. God painted the picture of His Church and it was full of brilliant skin colors and ages. Loneliness was never part of His plan. You will find these small communities everywhere. No wonder the media has labeled them "the church dispersed," for they are spreading out from the church walls to the streets of their cities, restoring the sense of community, fellowship, and rebuilding hope.

N. T. Wright describes a colorful church in *Simply Christian:*

> *It's a place of welcome and laughter; of healing and hope, of friends and family and justice and new life. It's where the homeless drop in for a bowl of soup and the elderly stop by for a chat. It's where one group is working to help drug addicts and an-*

other is campaigning for global justice. It's where you'll find people learning to pray, coming to faith, struggling with temptations, finding new purpose, and getting in touch with a new power to carry that purpose out. It's where people bring their own small faith and discover, in getting together with others to worship the one true God, that the whole becomes greater than the sum of its parts. [18]

Jesus knew the human struggle we face. That is why God sent the Holy Spirit to lead and guide and live within. Never alone, the human existence has taken on a very doable task. Surrendered to God, walking with Him, being His hands and feet to a hurting world takes on a glorious calling.

Now that's a place anyone could call home. The world is waiting for a place like this, for believers like this. Never underestimate the power of "just being" present in someone's life. Remember: determination does have a face, grace does have a place, and heroes, well, they have erasers and paintbrushes. They are called The UnStoppable Generation.

Saged UnStoppables Paint a Collage of Wisdom

*"Since my youth, O God, you have taught me,
and to this day I declare
your marvelous deeds.
Even when I am old and gray . . .
I declare your power to the next generation,
your might to all who are to come"*
(Psalm 71:17, 18, NIV).

The following is a montage of wisdom given to the younger of this UnStoppable Generation from the older ones. Given in broad strokes to encourage them; to show the world their true colors. Some are profound and some silly, but all have a point— on this UnStoppable journey, keep pointing to Jesus and follow Him all the days of your life.

~ God's grace forgives all our sins and they don't count in Heaven anymore. And because He loves us so much, He gave us erasers and paintbrushes for here on earth. Specially designed to erase our earthly, fleshly actions and paint new ones that reflect the beauty of Christ. It is a wonderful gift.

~ What a privilege it is to be in this timeline of God's history with you. As the younger among us, you must know that you inspire us and ignite the flame in many of us that was almost flickering out. We pray that our wisdom will impact your mind and cause you to stumble less than we did. So as we both journey together in this, our spot in time, let it be known that we were a bright light held with courage for our Lord's glory.

~ Don't you just love to imagine Jesus walking the dusty roads of Galilee? Or talking to his disciples in a boat? Or dream about what it will look like to see the Jesus of Revelation on a white horse. Funny, we act as if He is far off. When the truth is, He is here today, right in front of you. And if you know Him to be your Savior, then you have the privilege of having Him in you.

~ Jesus said, "The Kingdom of God has come." And guess what? He hasn't left.

~ COLOR OUTSIDE THE LINES.

~ For something to shine, it has to first be lit . . . strike a match!

~ God has a continuous flow of uniqueness. Never again will the world be like it is today. It is said that you can't step into a running river the same way twice.

Yet God is forever and always the same.

~ Stand for courage.

~ Great virtue is different from physical strength; it's inner strength.

~ What one generation tolerates, the next generation will embrace.

~ Fear is the pathway to surrender. To cover common fear you need but two things: truth and courage.

~ Make God's heart visible to a chaotic, cloudy, hurting world.

~ It's just not about you. Your provision and desires are not God's motivation. His glory is.

~ There are no off-limits places to share God's love.

~ Your life is the real estate perfect for the Kingdom to reside. And your heart is the perfect well. For out of it comes a Kingdom life flowing for all to see.

~ Carry the name. Not just theology . . . It's His name . . . talk about HIM! Talk about all books, or mission moves, or church plantings . . . talk about HIM!

~ You can't stand on any ground that isn't truly under your own feet.

~ What if you had the ability to influence the culture? What if you had in you the answer to someone else's question?

~ What roadblocks would you knock down; what obstacles would you go around to do what you were created to do?

PART TWO

HER GENDER:
Embracing Your Femininity

DRAMA 2

Traces of Eve in Me

"I'll be right over here. I just want to rest my feet," she hollered to her friend who was already well into the first store of the mall.

Glad for a break, she thought, *Ha!, what I really want is to rest my brain. This conference on being a woman of God has my head spinning. There is so much information that I haven't ever considered. I want to be a light for Christ; I want to reflect His glory. I want to learn how to do it like Grams. But I don't want to be weird. Grams wasn't weird.*

And what's all that talk about gifts and talents? I thought you had to give stuff up to do the God thing. I had no idea I was going to get something! I have so much to learn. I'm really glad there are two more days of lectures left. But frankly, from the sound of it, this could take me a lifetime.

She felt herself dozing off. As if in a fog, she thought she heard women talking.

Voices of the inheritance box, perhaps: "She's ... you know, that great cloud of witnesses."

"Weird? She doesn't look too weird."
— SWEET VOICE OF THE JUNE CLEAVER GENERATION

"We all looked a bit peculiar in our generations!"
— GIGGLING VOICE OF THE '20s FLAPPER

"I never did get it, and Sally over here got it late and

made a huge impact anyway. Her generation called her blessed."
— WILDERNESS WOMAN

"Not to worry, girls. That's my granddaughter; she'll figure out the right path."
— GRAMS

"Desire is the main thing."
— ROSIE THE RIVETER pipes in

"Ha! Yep! And fearlessness! She better not be a wimp!"
— AMERICAN FRONTIER WOMAN

"Be nice, girls. This li'l one . . . she just needs a little more info. Now stop your cackling, she's waking up."
— GRAMS

UGH! She stirred until fully awake. *I don't feel very fearless, so many thoughts in my head. I just don't want to think about anything for a while. I just want to sit here and people-watch.*
Silence. She begins to people-watch.
Hmmm . . . cute hair.
Nice purse.
Awful. That one's outfit does NOT match at all.
More watching continues.
That girl looks sad.
Why is that mother so angry? I feel guilty watching, but what's going on? I'll lean in a little closer. Hmmm . . . Argument over something . . . Lean in . . . clothes . . . yep, the swimsuit argument. Girl stomps off . . . typical.
Back to people-watching.
Wonder where she got that belt?
Wonder where that one got such an attitude?
I didn't know hips could move like that.

Whoa . . . talk about bossy. That one's ruling and running all over that poor guy.

Man, there are all kinds of women. That's what I was learning this morning at that lecture. My generation . . . Hmmm . . . they told us this morning . . . (She picks up her notes.)

Dictionary.com says:

Generation:

1) the entire body of individuals born and living at about the same time. 2) a group of individuals, most of whom are the same approximate age, having similar ideas, problems, attitudes

Pondering. She sits there, pondering.

Ha. Well, that describes this mall. But God is calling our generation to a whole different level.

Reading. She sits there reading her notes from the speaker.

The "She" side of the UnStoppable Generation

They are ageless and diverse. Living passionately in their timeslot of history. Fully feminine in design, yet each uniquely equipped with God-given gifts, talents, and paths. They have but one focus: to link arms with their brothers in Christ and fearlessly impact and imprint the world with God's love for God's Glory.

Pondering. She returns to pondering.

She . . . fearless? Strong? Ha. She better be.

At first I thought this movement was just a remix of feminism. Wow, did feminism ever mix things up! Somehow, equal pay ended up messing with our core design. Glad that's not what this is about. Those women just ended up angry and frustrated. I'm glad my generation is searching for the truth about gender. Seems simple, really, just being what God designed us to be, She and He. Being a She does not look like a He. It was never supposed to.

It's also not about being more powerful or excluding the He of our generation. Actually, it appears we are to be working together using our own designs to complement the "each other." That makes the best impact. Hmmm . . . and much more sense.

And another thing—why would God create two genders if one wasn't needed? He must know . . . duh... He's God.

(Cue far-off laughter of past She voices.)

"Now she's getting it."

Back to people-watching and pondering.

OK, OK. We absolutely should be working together impacting the world. Not the way the world sees it, but as God planned it. Hey, nice glasses . . . oops is that a girl or a boy?

Amused at herself, she continues wondering: *Glad the next session is all about gender. Wow, is that a common word lately! Everything I've heard from Oprah and 20/20 recently says that we need to get rid of gender, not to even tell our children if they are a boy or girl. Heard them say it is a better way to create a level playing field for everyone, so that in our sameness we can all thrive. Hmmm. That kind of sounds good, I guess, but it really just doesn't match how different we all are. I kind of like being different. The world and media seem to encourage the confusion, telling us we should wear the same clothes, drink the same coffee, and even use the same deodorant! Why do we buy into this? It seems to me that we all just want to belong. And belonging does NOT have to include sameness.*

Frustrated, she blurts out loud. "Ahhhh . . . here I go again, deep thinking . . . I just want to rest my brain."

Trying to distract herself, she decides to write down words that describe the way women interact with the men they are with. The list grows:

Moody
Pouting
Flirty
Sweet
Helping
Adoring
Manipulating
Seducing

Perplexed, she finds herself wondering: *The interaction in this mall could fill hundreds of books on gender.*

Suddenly she is brought back into full reality. "Ouch! You're pulling my arm!" she shrieks.

The arm tug is from her conference friend, back to retrieve her for the next session.

Out of breath, her friend says, "Come on . . . The escalator is over here; I don't want to be late. I heard the next section is on gender, and after being at this mall, I realize I could possibly be confused."

"Aha! You've been pondering too!"

"Plus, there's mayhem near the escalators."

"Why?"

"Stars from a new movie are waving to their worshipping fans."

"Quick! I see a path to get on. Looks like we are about to be lifted out of the confusion in more ways than one."

They both laugh as they slowly take the ride upward . . .

FIVE

The Issachar Equation

We are at a critical point in our culture. Some have called it a tipping point.

It seems that everything is being redefined, from the purpose of government to the description of marriage, and now the very essence of our gender.

Everyone is holding their breath waiting to see, hoping it will turn out OK. Everyone that is—except God. He knew this generation would come, and He knew the confusion the redefining would cause. He isn't surprised or blown away by the stats or the crazy new definitions man has devised. In fact, long before time began, He set into place a remnant of people for each generation that would hold fast to His true design in their spot of time.

Those people would know Him and provide answers.

Now, the same God who blew life into the first woman is now breathing life into her daughters. They may have had the life knocked out of them in recent decades, but there is a wind blowing across this nation that is reviving her again. It is the fragrance that can only be defined as beautifully feminine.

"Feminism" has been with us for 50 years now, and many are wondering if the ol' girl needs a makeover. Women who are angry, bitter, and hate men just aren't the norm anymore. S.E. Coup, in a political analysis, expounds on the question in *Carolina Journal*—"Has Feminism Outlived its Usefulness?":

> *The kind of rhetoric—anti-man, anti-state, anti-family—that lacks the resonance it probably once had. Now it just sounds dated and bitter, and especially to women in my generation. I have to assume to women in [college] as well. I mean, it sounds foreign to me. Women of my generation, especially conservative women, believe that feminism's ultimate success is that we don't need it anymore. We're women who see any initiative that separates the sexes as sexist, not feminist. We're women who are uncomfortable with being positioned as victims of anything, let alone of our gender. We're women who believe that men are just as qualified to speak about the importance of women's issues as women are— that propping women up by pushing men down is an insult to our fathers and uncles, brothers and mentors and all the men who have helped us along the way.[19]*

Yet there are those who want to hold on to the self-defining theory and redefine things once again. Oprah's website writer, Karen Salmansohn, had an idea for the name change in her article, "Are You a Feminist or a Feminine-ist?"

> *These are words men can and should stand by, and stand for, in their own lives. I can definitely envision my fiancé proudly calling himself a 'feminine-ist'*

because he's in touch with both his feminine and masculine sides, and he loves when I am able to tap into this dynamic duo of sexiness and powerfulness in myself.[20]

OK, but, does that really clear things up? No. Really, no matter what it's called, is there another option other than feminism? From carpool lines to college campuses, the masses are curious. And with everyone taking random stabs at it, things could be getting more confusing before they clear up. Perhaps it is time to check with someone who has some authority.

Biblical Womanhood

Biblical womanhood is a new phrase that has hit the gender-defining conversation. But the concept is as old as time itself. So what's all this talk about biblical womanhood and femininity? Women of all ages are leaning in a little closer, hoping that there will be an answer they can understand and actually do. Even in the churches, looking for answers, they are secretly embarrassed that they can't define their own gender. What's left is a generation of women wondering and hoping there is more to their gender than what the world proclaims. Longingly, they are asking questions like:

- Who is "she"?
- Is her femininity a strength or a sorrow?
- Is gender something that should be embraced or erased?
- What does it even look like lived out, and does it even matter?

The answer to that last one is a resounding YES. It really *does* matter. There is a purpose and there is a plan. It is real and it exists. Women should be saying to each other:

"Get excited, girl, we really are more than we ever imagined!"

Assuming you are a believer and you count yourself as part of the UnStoppable Generation, the discussion about gender may not be anything new. You most likely have heard the banter and read the debates, the random declarations and theories about being a woman or a man. Or not being a man or woman or . . . let's just call it a draw and forget trying to figure it out, some would say.

But what about you? Do you know what God thinks about your womanhood? You are about to find out in this section. And it is of vital importance that you do. Not because it's so incredible—even if it is—but also because, as an UnStoppable, you are "the men of Issachar" to your generation.

"From Issachar, men who understood the times and knew what Israel should do" (1 Chronicles 12:32, NIV).

But I'm not a man, you say. You're also not living in the Old Testament. God's Word has always been applicable and relevant for every generation. No matter the gender or timeslot, it is full of powerful promises. For God is the same yesterday, today, and tomorrow. His Word is truth and light for anyone who is looking for either.

The Men of Issachar

These men were a small group of leaders that served Israel in a time of national crisis. They were men that knew the Word of God. They were not just a little familiar with it; they *understood* it. Uniquely, they also had a firm grasp on the times they lived in. They knew the condition of the nation, why the people were struggling, and they could see the destruction that was ensuing. They weren't just off in a temple somewhere reading Scripture and praying.

These were men who were on the street. Just like you, UnStoppable. They had hands-on experience with what was happening to the people. Knowing the Word and understanding the times in which they lived provided these men with something that no one else had—wisdom.

They were the perfect equation: they knew the Word, they understood the times they lived in, and so . . . they could tell Israel what to do.

The Isscahar equation is one that still computes in today's society. It is the nature of an UnStoppable to be out where the people are. Effective problem-solvers, they don't have any trouble stepping out of the box if it is for God. However, no matter how much they desire to solve the problems of the world, if they don't follow the Issachar equation and don't know what the Bible says, they could be deceived.

Effective problem-solvers, they don't have any trouble stepping out of the box if it is for God.

It is to this end that this section of the book is written. To provide UnStoppable women with the knowledge of what God says about their womanhood. While we will not be addressing biblical manhood directly, we will be addressing biblical gender principals. It is hoped that these chapters will begin to unravel some of the misinterpretations and lies about our design as men and women. Equipping you with the knowledge to live the Issachar equation, so that the Word of God would capture hearts and triumph in these days.

Are you ready? Ready to live like God created you to live? It will surely be counter-cultural; some have called it revolutionary. But that's OK. UnStoppables are known for their trail-blazing. Saddle up.

SIX

No More Cookie Cutters

No more cookie cutters. PLEASE! The 1950s . . . sappy, sweet pearls and aprons. The 1960s . . . an angry, bra-burning feminist, stomping on men. The Victoria Secret models, or high-powered career women. Now, there is one for biblical womanhood? Ugh. Will the redefining ever end? Don't be embarrassed that you're frustrated. You are not the only one tired of the checklist to be the perfect this or that. Not to mention the constant media reminder to pick up your next role model from the world, magazines, and Hollywood.

You tell yourself that you're an UnStoppable and that you break molds you don't fit in. Have you heard yourself scream, "I just want to be ME!"?

You are not alone. Women all over this country are saying that enough is enough. Pleading: "Would someone *please* just get the definition right so we can move on!" They don't want to remix how to be a woman again. And if you listen closely, you might hear the Spirit of God whispering in quiet excitement: *"Really? Are you really done looking outside? Because I'd like to show you the wonder of your womanhood, the authentic you."*

Getting Some Things Straight Before the Big 'Redefine'

As society heads into the process of redefining gender, there are a few definitions that need to be established first if gender is to be defined correctly. One of the words that can get things stuck is the deceiving little prefix "re."

> **re** – *to do again; implying direction, place, or position of time; to go back and do again*[21]

· · · · · · · · · · · · · · · · · ·

Would someone please just get the definition right so we can go on!

· · · · · · · · · · · · · · · · · ·

This definition might give some insight into the redefining problem. For if "re" means you go back to a position in time to find the definition, then how far back do you go? Back in time to wherever you want to stop? 1960, 1920, the Victorian Age? It is very subjective and can only continue the confusion of defining. Unfortunately, all those eras defined womanhood in one way or another—only to find out that they did not have the real answer.

Is a Real Answer Really Real?

Real — to be true and actual; not imaginary

Real is subjective. For instance, someone might have a 4-carat Cubic Zirconia diamond ring. When asked if it is real, they could reply, yes. Technically, according to the definition of "real," a CZ diamond ring is "not imaginary"—it is actual, so you could say, loosely, that it is real.

But if asked if the diamond is authentic, the only truthful answer would have to be, no it is not.

The Power of Authentic

Words mean things, and in this journey to find truth, we need to make sure we are on the right track. The only way for the redefining of gender to be accurate and never have to be remixed again is for us to "re": go back and find the authentic, original definition and start there.

> *Authentic*: Having a claimed and verifiable origin or authorship; not counterfeit or copied

> *Original*: the first and genuine form of something from which others are derived [22]

This lesson in terms will be what is needed for a true conclusion to be reached. It is essential that we do not just redefine womanhood to our liking; we must be diligent and honest to define it authentically, or we have only served to deceive yet another generation.

Therefore, as we have unpacked meaning from the terms above, we must conclude:

A redefining definition cannot be someone's opinion, or formed to fit a platform. It must be able to be proven as authentic. And only from the original can the basis of an authentic definition be concluded.

Authentic Womanhood

Can the authentic, original design of womanhood be located? The answer is yes. It is found in the Bible. Counter to the culture of feminism, the Bible has the only record of the original design of man and woman. The rest of the definitions are theories, opinions, or philosophies.

It is also important at this point to note that feminism is not a definition of a woman; it is a philosophy lived out by women. Big difference. Any word ending in "ism" is defined as:

> **ism** – *a distinctive doctrine, theory, system, philosophy; typically a political ideology.*[23]

A Place to Stand

In the garden God had a plan
To display himself through the creation of man
One's not enough it would definitely take two.
To reflect all He was to a world oh so new.
The design was perfect it fit like a glove
Each of equal value equally felt His love
Uniquely woman and uniquely man
The two reflecting one, living in God's land
From the garden through time, no one thought it untrue
Until one generation demanded their own point of view.
Discontent and angry and pulling out their hair
They shouted: I am a woman and I want things to be fair.
They tossed out the role of woman, thought it best to be a man.
God said you can't do that. They said, Oh yes we can.
It sounded fair and it sounded good.
Now no one sees each other or God like they should.
Confusion abounds, no one knows where to stand
Perhaps we should reconsider God's master plan. [24]
— M.C.

I am so glad to find that God didn't cram us into a cookie cutter mold demanding that we stay put and fit right into it. Instead, he lovingly formed us as a potter forms a precious piece of china. It really doesn't matter if the culture of any "ism" changes the definitions or not.

The authentic has already been designed. Our womanhood and manhood have been placed in his grand design and are destined to be authentic for all time. Truth is still truth even if someone denies the very existence of it.

God has all the answers, and He isn't hiding them from anyone. His desire is that we would see the wonder of why He created us male and female. So now let's move onward in our word-journey to discover the beautiful truth of authentic womanhood.

UnStoppable, this is going to rock your world.

SEVEN

The Mystery Revealed

Everyone loves a good mystery and the Bible is a great source for stories. However, the Scriptures aren't fairy tales or a great script that God thought up to communicate truth to us. It is real and it really happened. You know the disclaimer you see at the beginning of a movie that looks something like this:

> *"The names of the people in this feature film have been changed to protect the innocent . . . "*

Well, God doesn't do that. The people within the pages of the Bible are real and their names are real. God doesn't protect us from seeing sin. He wants us to expose it so we can learn from it. He is all about truth, because He is truth.

As part of the UnStoppable generation, it is probable that you hold the Bible as the ultimate source of truth for your life and your future. But let's just stay on our steady truth-journey and state some facts about why the Bible has the original, authentic truth that makes it the final authority. J. Steve Lee, Bible teacher and scholar, in an apologetics pamphlet, gives just a few.

- Dates: Early dating shows eyewitnesses were alive during the time the text was written. The time was too short for legends to develop. It takes at least two generations for a legend to develop.
- Manuscript evidence/Number of manuscript copies: The New Testament itself has more manuscripts than any other ancient document with more than 5,745. Homer's *Iliad* had 643; some Plato documents had 49 copies; Aristotle, seven copies.
- Archaeological evidence: Dead Sea Scrolls found in 1947 in Qumran, Israel provided the oldest copies of almost all of the books of the Old Testament, confirming the reliability of transmission process. Also other locations unearthed to prove the existence of Scripture references.

John McRay, professor of New Testament and archaeology, author of *Archaeology and the New Testament*. Supervised excavations at Caesarea, Sepphoris, and Herodium. John McRay has stated: "Archaeology has not produced anything that is unequivocally a contradiction to the Bible. And there is no question that the credibility of the New Testament is enhanced through archaeology."[25]

Of course there are many more, and a quick look at the references in the back of the book will guide you further. It is important to know why you believe what you believe. After all, if you are living your life based on the Word of God, then you really should know that what you know really is authentic.

The Book That Speaks

We have already learned that words mean powerful things, and God's words are powerfully packed between its covers. Hebrew 4:12 defines it perfectly:

> *"For the word of God is alive and powerful. It is sharper than the sharpest two-edged sword, cutting between soul and spirit, between joint and marrow. It exposes our innermost thoughts and desires"* (NLT).

An amazing book, the Bible is written with two kingdoms in view: God's heavenly Kingdom and man's earthly kingdom. God works in both the physical and the spiritual. And His stories always have a little of both in them. Reading them is like unveiling a mystery that has precious jewels hidden all over the place. One just needs to dig in and discover them. The Bible: one God, one Book, two worlds.

In the Beginning . . .

You might be wondering why all these facts and Scriptures when you just want a definition of biblical womanhood. It is because knowledge of the Word is essential to the Issachar Equation so that you, UnStoppable, will be equipped in the Word, understand the times you live in, and be able to share truth with your generation. So don't skip over this story even if you think you already know it. Read it again with a fresh heart and see the Lord working wonders as He creates the original you.

The *Dunamis* Words of God

Before God even created man and woman, He was using some pretty powerful words that had a powerful effect on the world. The word *dunamis* is often used to describe the power of God and His words.

Dunamis is the Greek word from which we get our word *dynamite*.[26] Enough said.

Genesis 1 finds God creating.

And God said . . . let there be light

And there was light.

And God said . . . let there be fish.

And there were fish.

And God said . . . And God said . . . and God said.

I don't mean to be simplistic, but basically . . . God said, and it was what He said.

His words aren't super-intellectual as we read them today, or, maybe, they don't even sound spiritual. They weren't a chant or an incantation, although . . . it must have been spectacular. He just called it as what it was to be, and it became that thing. Wow. This is an astounding revelation; God really is powerful. He doesn't just design things, He calls them into being.

It Happened in a Garden

The story continues and moves into the Garden of Eden. God has spoken everything into existence and He now prepares to do something miraculous. The movement of the tense language slows down as if God is contemplating with anticipation what is next. Can you imagine in your mind's eye what it looked like? The angels just waiting for what on earth He would do next after the amazing five days of creating the heavens and the earth. God pauses.

There is no question what He plans to do. He has been thinking about this long before the foundations of the world were laid. He knows the implications and the joy that will ensue. The conversation is taking place among the Trinity: Father, Son, and Holy Spirit. And it is with that dynamic relationship in mind that He speaks.

"Let us make man in our own image, after our likeness. And let them have dominion over the fish of the sea and over the birds of the heavens and over the livestock and over all the earth and over every creeping thing that creeps on the earth. So God created man in his own image, in the image of God he created him; male and female he created them" (Genesis 1:26, 27, ESV).

Then God did something He had not done during all the creating.

"God formed the man from the dust of the ground and breathed into his nostrils the breath of life and man became a living being" (Genesis 2:7, NIV).

Imagine the wonder of it! The God who could speak anything into existence reaches down to form man with His own hands, then with love and pleasure in his design, He lovingly breathes His very own life into that man. Can you see the limp form come to life in your mind?

What was the interaction like as Creator God met the eyes of the created man? That is something we will be able to ask in Heaven one day, but for now we must rely on the Scriptures. Then God did one last thing on the sixth day of creation. He created woman.

Listen as God brings Adam all the animals to name.

"And Adam gave names to all the livestock and to the birds of the air and to every beast of the field; but for Adam there was not found a helper suitable, adapted, complementary for him. So the Lord caused a deep sleep to fall upon Adam; and while he was asleep He took one of his ribs and closed up the place with flesh. And the rib or part of his side which the lord God had taken from the man he fashioned and made into a woman, and He brought her to the man" (Genesis 2:20-22, AMP).

Oh the wonder of the moment, as God provides a bride for Adam. Adam immediately sees that she is like him and quickly names her *woman*, for she came out of man. They were separate, but God was about to bring them together in marriage as one.

> *"That is why a man leaves his father and mother and is united to his wife, and they become one flesh"* (Genesis 2:24, NIV).

What a day the sixth day had been! No wonder they all rested on the seventh day.

God, satisfied in His completed work. A deep joy seeing Himself gloried through His creation. God had done it all. There was no striving for man or woman. They just showed up on the sixth day; they were not the creator, they were the creation that simply walked without effort into the grace-filled life God had created for them. They were grateful to spend the day glorifying and worshipping the God who showed his glory through their creation. And it was very good.

Don't you just love a good story? And that was just the beginning of what God had planned long before time even began. Our gender was not an afterthought to God. He knew that as He created man and woman He would hide a mystery within them and their story. Purposefully, manhood and womanhood would foreshadow something wonderful. It was hinted at throughout the Old Testament but would not be revealed until Christ died on the cross.

The book of Ephesians would eventually connect the dots for us. It is through the work of Jesus Christ and His love for the church that the mystery is revealed. It brings into perfect view the relationship of man, woman, sexuality, and marriage, which is the beautiful reflection of Christ, His church, and the relationship between them.

A word to singles: Remember, you are still the church.

And as a man or woman, you still hold fast to the gift of your manhood or womanhood. The apostle Paul loved his singleness, it freed him to be radical in his serving. For though marriage is meant to display the glory of Christ with the Church, there are Kingdom truths that can be radiated more clearly through singleness than marriage. Such as: Singleness shows that God's family is not multiplied through sexual intercourse, but through faith in Christ. It also bears witness that relationships in Christ are more permanent that those of biological families.

Manhood/Womanhood: Gender-Equal, Yet Different

When God created male and female, He did so with great intent. Within the beautiful masterpiece of gender was hidden a mystery that would be revealed in his timing. The arguing over which is strongest or better is futile. For both are equally loved, both equally valued, and both intentionally designed with purpose.

Mary Kassian and Nancy Leigh DeMoss describe this wonderful combination in their *True Woman 101: Divine Design* Bible study, by Moody Publishing.

> *The ponderosa pine has intricately grooved orangey-brown bark, long slender needles, and a faint vanilla smell. The bark of the Douglas fir is dark*

The arguing over which is strongest or better is futile. For both are equally loved, both equally valued, and both intentionally designed with purpose.

and deeply furrowed. Its flat, pointy needles spiral around each twig. The smell is distinctively strong and earthy. Each type of tree is beautiful in and of itself. But when viewed together-as a forest surrounded by peaks and valleys, sparkling rivers, and a vast expanse of cornflower blue sky the rich green carpet of trees is absolutely gorgeous . . . . Wouldn't it be silly for the ponderosa pine and the Douglas fir to get into a debate about which type of tree is more vital to the forest? They are different and equal. Neither is better than the other. But sadly, this is what often happens between men and women.

Genders and roles are specific for a reason. They reflect God to a world that can't see him. And even more magnificently, genders and marriage put the Gospel on display.

Man: Designed to reflect Christ's strength, self-sacrifice, and His love for the bride—eternal love for her—and to provide and protect and help her become all God created her to be. To pursue and protect her, sacrificing himself for her, even unto death.

Woman: Designed to reflect the responsiveness of the redeemed with love and admiration, displaying the beauty of the bride. To bring life, and tender care, to assist him, abiding, devoted to him, to work with him in reaching the world for the sake of the Gospel, and to love him with an abandoned heart.

Marriage: Designed to reflect the covenant of Christ and the church. The promise that as man and woman become one, so does Christ and the church. As a father gives away the bride at a wedding, likewise Father God gives the church to the groom, Christ.

The story continues to this very day. Displaying his powerful redemptive plan through mankind isn't about us, it is about Him. We glorify Him as we journey into our fallen world, sharing and being the hands of Christ. Looking forward to the story's end that is spoken of in the New Testament book of Revelation. When Christ will return for his bride, the church, and we will all take our place at the marriage supper table.

All of this puts manhood and womanhood at the center of God's plan to show the world the magnificent Gospel.

This marvelous story is not just a good analogy that God thought of long after creating us. Like, "Hey, that creation story would be good to compare to my Son's provision of salvation." No. He didn't look at manhood and woman-hood as a helpful comparison to Christ and the church. He knew before time began, before He created the first light of dawn, that the rebellion and sin of man would require redemption and the death of his Son to redeem His lost bride.

He created manhood and womanhood with purpose. So that through all time, and every generation, there would be a visible display in the human body and cov-enant relationship that could not be denied. Therefore, God created manhood and womanhood specifically different and, ultimately, to put on display the power of who He is and the wonder of His glory.

So, sweet UnStoppable, you now know why your wom-anhood is so valuable and why it is such a privilege to be hand-fashioned by the Creator. Therefore, the true, authentic definition of your womanhood is . . .

True Womanhood

A distinctive calling by God to display the glory of his Son in ways that would not be displayed if there were no womanhood. — John Piper[27]

Go ahead, take a minute to read that again and relish the thoughts that are too wonderful to imagine. We will discuss how that looks in your life in the final section. But for now, just soak in the authentic truth of God's love and design for your womanhood. Tissues may be necessary.

EIGHT

Hunger Like Starvation

Ever watch a thrilling movie for the second time and, just when the most awful part is about to happen, you want to warn the characters of impending doom, and you find yourself yelling out loud: "Don't do it, please don't do it!" But you remember it's a movie and, deflated, you watch as "they" do it again.

That's how it can feel reading Genesis 3. You know the story: the Garden of Eden, the woman, the snake, and that luscious fruit.

Let's take a peek at the real-life story again, and it's OK if you want to yell in the . . . well, you know which part.

The New Living Translation unfolds the drama for us as we read Genesis 3:1-7.

> *"The serpent was the shrewdest of all the wild animals the LORD God had made. One day he asked the woman, 'Did God really say you must not eat*

the fruit from any of the trees in the garden?'

"'Of course we may eat fruit from the trees in the garden,' the woman replied.

"'It's only the fruit from the tree in the middle of the garden that we are not allowed to eat. God said, "You must not eat it or even touch it; if you do, you will die."'

"'You won't die!' the serpent replied to the woman. 'God knows that your eyes will be opened as soon as you eat it, and you will be like God, knowing both good and evil.'"

"The woman was convinced. She saw that the tree was beautiful and its fruit looked delicious, and she wanted the wisdom it would give her. So she took some of the fruit and ate it. Then she gave some to her husband, who was with her, and he ate it, too.

"At that moment their eyes were opened, and they suddenly felt shame at their nakedness. So they sewed fig leaves together to cover themselves."

. . . And she ate it. Don't you hate that part? Don't you feel sorry for Eve? Not only will her own life be filled with the regret of that mistake, but for all time she will be labeled as the "one that bit the apple." By the way, the Bible doesn't identify it as an apple, but only refers to it as "fruit." Yet, even to this day, the sight of an apple with a bite out of it reminds you of Eve and her choice.

Why did that fruit cause her so much temptation? Was she just super hungry? Or just feeling a little too big for her . . . um, well, guess she didn't have britches. Or just feeling a little left out, untaken care of, discontented with the rules that God had made.

She knew what God had said; she even quoted Him perfectly. But the serpent tried a second time and he snagged her attention. Suggesting that God was holding out on her, that God knew that the tree of knowledge had good and evil. He knew what all that was about, that good-and-evil stuff. Why couldn't she take it? If she was made in his image, why didn't she know what that good and evil knowledge was? Can't you just see her running it all through her head? Then the New Living Translation says, "She was convinced." She had considered all that was in front of her and she was convinced. Unfortunately, she had not considered the consequences. She just wanted what she wanted.

Standing next to her. Close enough to receive the piece of fruit, possibly an apple. Adam. His silence speaks to his considering and final choice to also disobey God and eat the fruit. He too did not think of the consequences. He just didn't want to take the authority. Authority that was his; God himself had given it to both of them. Adam was the husband and had the influence to stop Eve as she stood there contemplating. He also had authority over the serpent, the devil. He could have set that slimy, lying snake straight by saying "No, we will obey God. You get out of here and stay away from my wife!"

But he didn't, and the result was disobedience in God's eyes.

So, Eve—whose name means "life giver"—became a "life destroyer." She gave the fruit to her husband and he ate it too. They got what they wanted. They had already known good, but now they knew evil. God had spoken truth about the tree. And the evil that was found was their own, the sin of selfishness and pride. They also soon found that ducking and covering wasn't going to work, for although they had believed what the serpent said about becoming like God, they had not factored in that the enemy of their souls was a liar. God was still God, and they were not. That fruit of rebellion against the truth of God caused a curse and death to come to them and all mankind after them. It was a sin they could not fix or repay; they were put out of the Garden with curses intact.

But God loved them so much. Long before their creation He knew this moment would come. So He set into motion the happy ending for all mankind when he would send Jesus to pay for that sin. He would be born to a virgin.

Fast forward to Mary, another woman who also had a choice. Let's look in on the scene as she is introduced to God's will for her life.

This true story does not open in a beautiful garden but in a dusty, poor town called Nazareth. Mary is a young virgin, about to be married. Life is going as planned, until the angel, Gabriel, shows up to tell her that she has been chosen to be the mother of the Savior, Christ Jesus. She stops in her sandals and considers what she had just heard from God. She has a question about how. (God doesn't mind our questions.) She must have considered the reactions she would face from being an unwed mother; who would believe her, and would things turn out all right? (There is wisdom to weighing the fact.) Then she made her choice. To believe God's word and trust Him as she responded:

> *"For nothing is impossible with God. Mary responded, 'I am the Lord's servant. May everything you have said about me come true'"* (Luke 1:37, NLT).

Eve and Mary: two women, two choices, and two very different outcomes.

Hunger That Felt Like Starvation

The common thread both Eve and Mary had was a hunger that felt like starvation, a hunger that they could not control. One would turn the world to death, and the other would bring life to that same world.

Eve: She was the original life giver, so how did she end up feeding death to the whole human race?

~ She choose to use her apple to nourish her self and brought sin into the beautiful garden.

~ She used her feminine design to influence her husband for evil.

~ She became a taker instead of a giver.

~ A hunger for knowledge that longed to take what belonged to God. Like starvation, she wanted it so bad. She saw it could be hers, and in her selfishness she said, Yes I can. And she did. Sad thing; she was never satisfied.

~ The apple was rotten and the smell of sin is still with us today.

Mary: Also a life giver, she had a hunger that felt like starvation too. Mary, whose words whispered wonderful things; she died to self and chose God's truth for her life.

~ She had the privilege of feeling the Savior kick her tummy.

~ To watch Him toddle around and tuck Him in at night.

~ She had the privilege of watching Him give His life as the sacrifice for all sin, including her own.

~ She hungered for knowing God. A hunger that seemed like starvation was satisfied through dying to self and surrendering to Him, trusting Him with the outcome.

~ Her surrendered life brought a harvest called the church, and it is a sweet fragrance to God.

Heart Check

UnStoppable, you wouldn't be this far into this book if you didn't want to know what God thinks. So, now would be a good time for you to check your motives. Where does your hunger lie? Are you a life giver when you speak in your school, job, or family? Take a moment and ask God to reveal any area that might be producing stinky, rotten fruit and sucking the life out of those around you.

The Curse of Eve

Eve's hunger to control caused her more than exile from the Garden. She received a curse in her body that would be passed from generation to generation. The curse was specific to her gender and to her sin.

Eve, who had delivered death to mankind, would now have pain in childbirth. And because she tried to take authority from God and her husband, she would forever fight the desire to control, manipulate, and dominate everything, especially man.

This curse is with us even now. Just ask a pregnant woman or one who has a newborn. The pain is still part of our lives. And what about the desire to dominate? Just spend time in a committee of women trying to decide something. The curse of Eve almost always shows up. Control and manipulation is something all women fight. Even ones like Mary and you, too, who love the Lord, fight to die to self and surrender.

Hunger to Control

The desire to control is stronger than ever in our culture. Eve's curse has traveled far and even gained strength in our society as the feminist movement came on the scene. God was deemed unwanted and unnecessary. Self was once again hungry to take truth into its hands.

"We as women need and can trust NO other authority than our own personal truth."
—Betty Friedan, founder of the Feminist Movement [28]

The "new freedoms" that were grabbed left a generation entirely self-focused instead of others-focused. Self-things rarely work. We were created for relationships. It is when we are others-minded that our needs are satisfied. I help fulfill yours and you help fulfill mine.

For example:

~ Compassion toward you. You feel heard and understood. Life.

~ Compassion inward, to self, is uncomforted self-pity. Death.

~ Love to others brings joy to you. Life.

~ Self-love brings frustration of never having enough. Death.

Heart Check: This is a hard check, but it must be done. Take heart; we all have to assess the damage of the curse of Eve in our lives. Challenge yourself to honor the men in your life—your husband, father, and brothers. Watch for the moments that you control or manipulate your sisters or children. A great start would be to study humility. *Humility* by CJ Mahaney or *I Am Not, But I Know I AM*, by Louie Giglio, are good places to begin.

Blessings Satisfied

We, as daughters of Eve, must look at the apple in front of us every day. Will we decide to be like Mary and die to ourselves and our plans and trust God for what He has set before us? Actually, things turned out very well for Mary; they call her blessed. In her obedience she ended up as the most famous mother of all time.

Even today, Eve receives our "Oh girl, you really shouldn't have," while Mary receives our "Girl, so glad you did."

Which one will you pick?

Bad Girls/Good Girls

It is very important to know that God loved Eve as much as He loved Mary. He had formed Eve and fashioned her so tenderly. It must have been sad for God to see her fall. But it was not her actions of disobedience that would be a measurement of His love. He loved her with the same unconditional, eternal love with which He also loved Mary. And Mary, in her obedience, did not receive more love for choosing a good path. For before and after her decision, God loved her with the same love that he lavished on Eve. Their choices produced a different earthly outcome. But in Heaven, God's love was perfectly intact.

God is not mad at you, nor was he at Eve.

And that goes for you too. Let's face it: God is not mad at you, nor was He at Eve, for that matter. God cannot love you more than He did from the beginning. There is nothing you could ever do super-right or terribly wrong—even if it was worse than a sin like . . . biting that apple, and we all agree that was really bad. His love for them and for you is never based on actions. And the wonderful part is, you can know and experience this love personally. You only need to see your behavior as sin, ask for forgiveness, and receive His gift of salvation. What a God! What Love!

Speak Life

UnStoppable, you are the one many have been waiting for. Speak life into the deepest, darkest spots of the world. Then you will be living as the life giver you were designed to be. A woman who exemplifies the words of Toby Mac's song,

"Speak Life"
Well it's crazy to imagine,
Words from our lips as the arms of compassion,
Mountains crumble with every syllable.
Hope can live or die.
Look into the eyes of the brokenhearted,
Watch them come alive as soon as you speak hope,
you speak love, you speak life.[29]

Show the grace-filled mercy that God showed you, to all you meet, even to those Eves who still like the curse. And most of all, walk humbly with God, surrendering your life to Him. Die to your self-ways, and watch as God pours your life out as a beautiful feminine fragrance that honors him.

Good-Bye

The alabaster bottle was broken it fell on the floor.
The perfume inside didn't need it any more.
The fragrance ran through the atmosphere so quick.
The broken bottle, all in pieces, no one noticed it.
It was broken, not needed, its purpose was done.
The perfume had another life living for God's Son.
A life before Christ is this picture I made.
Tells my own "bottle" story of how I got saved.
Conviction of sin came clear in my mind.
I repented and believed and called Jesus mine.
Though the old me is trashed, old habits pop up.
My soul can go sin searching in the grim and the muck.
I scream to myself, what are you doing? Beware.
That old life is gone you don't want it repaired.
Quit picking up pieces to keep and to mend.
They hold no good purpose, not a friend in the end.
Stop trying to mend the sin and strife.
Die to it already! Get on with your life!
At times I miss it, my bottle before.
But then I remember the One I adore.
Broken bottle not needed, I am brand new.
My life is in Christ, His fragrance mine too.
The Spirit's soft oil, soaks me clear through.
Good-bye broken life, I have died to you.[30]
— M.C.

PART THREE

HER GRIT:
Living the UnStoppable Life

DRAMA 3

The Fragrance

"Let's just duck into a store and let the parking lot clear out before we head home."

She had barely heard her friend say the words, and then she responded, "All this talk about being a sweet, feminine fragrance of Christ to the world around me has me wondering what I smell like."

The conference had shaken both their worlds. Her best friend was more joyful than see had seen her in years. "Well, we have been at this for three days," her friend answered as she smelled her own shirt. "Maybe we should go to the fancy store and get something exquisite," she laughed. "On second thought, you go and I'll run and get the car. Your head is in the clouds anyway. Go, and watch where you're walking," she hollered as she passed through the swinging mall doors.

She found herself thinking deeply. "Hmmm, good idea: a new perfume for my new life as an UnStoppable She."

Just then, a serious yet sweet saleswoman approached. "Hi, my name is Olga."

Noticing her accent she asked, "Where are you from?"

"Russia," Olga said, trying to sound more American.

She almost giggled. "Um, I didn't think Russians wore a lot of perfume."

The woman's face softened. "Oh dear, we Russians are famous for the depth of our scents. What is it you are looking for? A cologne or a perfume?"

"What's the difference? I have never bought expensive perfume . . . um, or cologne."

"O dear . . . cologne is plentiful and can be a bit ordinary. But a perfume . . . " Olga's voice slowed as she leaned in. "It is concentrated with the finest ingredients and comes with a great cost. Here, try one of these."

Olga proceeded through a series of about ten different bottles. In true sales form she held each one up, announcing its name and then the essence each one had and what others would think about you if you chose to purchase it. Olga was in true sales mode, showing she had done this many times that day.

"This one is a very sexy one; do you want to be seen as sexy?"

"Night at the opera. Very heavy for the elegant woman."

"All business. Not too much until they get really close . . . "

"Are you the, I-am-woman type, dominating type?" Olga quizzed.

Not waiting for an answer, Olga continued with colognes named Guilty, Naughty, Angel/Demon, and Obsession.

Sounds cheap and fast to me, she thought to herself.

She then realized that Olga was trying to find out who she was and what she wanted others to see her as. Still, she was thinking: *Ha. This sweet sales lady is trying to figure out who and what I am . . . She has no clue and, to tell you the truth, I'm just figuring it out myself.*

Olga tried harder as left the colognes and took her over to the finest of perfumes.

"Now this line of perfume has names for each scent that tell a story of love," Olga piped up.

Now she had her attention. Names like:

Chance Meeting
Falling in Love
Touch of Heaven
Betrayal

Revenge

"Can't stop thinking about the love story of Christ." She tried to clap her hand over her mouth, but it was too late—Olga had heard her talking out loud.

A quizzical look was on Olga's face.

Thinking she already looked silly, she just finished her thought process out loud, hoping she would make sense. "And all He has done for the bride, His church. And how our genders reflect the relationship between each other and Jesus and the bride. . . . I guess there isn't a perfume to put on to reflect that?"

Too late. Olga, who surely thought her crazy, was walking past her.

But to her surprise, Olga crooked her index finger and said, "Oh, sweet one, there is. Come with me."

As they were walking to the back of the room, Olga said, "I noticed you when you came in. I had a feeling you weren't looking to define yourself through a scent. I too am a believer. I love my job. It is my mission ground; I am able to talk to women and encourage them to do more than wear a fragrance, but to be one, and then I tell them about Christ."

She continued to tell her about the women she encountered. "Some want their cologne to scream out that they are female and on the hunt. Always too much perfume, those girls; you can smell them a block away. Then there are the ones that hug you and think you will remember them after they leave.

"So, they put the cologne all over their clothes, and then it's all over yours, too."

Her speech slowed again. "But the one that puts the purest form of perfume inside on their skin, close to their hearts, they are the ones that—as you get close—you can smell the wonder of them, and when they draw back, the fragrance draws you forward, back to them again. You desire to enjoy the scent, for it is soft and inviting, not harsh, or brash, not in-your-face, up-your-nose, and certainly not on your clothes," she giggled.

As she continued, she had a far off look in her eyes, "I like to think we have a spiritual scent that draws others to us. As we put on the love of Christ we are a sweet aroma that is gentle and inviting, and those around us experience Him."

Following her past the flashy promotional signs, they arrived behind a counter.

"Over here," Olga whispered with intrigue.

The anticipation was thick as Olga reached in a drawer and pulled out an old wooden box that held a black velvet bag. From the bag, she tenderly lifted out a beautiful crystal bottle. The bottle was truly magnificent, but what was inside it took her breath away. There within that bottle was a liquid that was shimmering and glistening. It was the purest pink she had ever seen.

"Oh my, what is that?" she said in a whisper.

Proudly, Olga announced, "This sweet one is from my Russian ancestors. It has been passed down for generations through the women in my family."

She smiled, thinking of her own inheritance box still sitting in her kitchen. She was sure it didn't smell as good as this bottle would.

Olga continued. "It is to be used only by women in our line, and especially on the day of her wedding, when it is time for her to be a bride."

"What color is that? I've never seen a pink like that," she said.

Olga nodded in agreement and continued her story. "Oh, that is because it's made from the finest ingredients. The reddest roses that represent the blood of Christ. The whitest of jasmine representing His church, righteous and pure. And it isn't just the ingredients that make this so wonderful." She paused and leaned closer.

"It is the method in which the fragrance is made. See if

you can envision the spiritual side of it all," Olga said as she slowly unfolded a yellowed piece of paper that told a tale that she knew she would be telling her children for years.

Then, cradling the paper gently in her hands, Olga reverently began to read it out loud.

Holder of the bottle,
You hold in your hand a mixture of wonder and beauty
that belongs to all who belong to Christ and desire to be a
fragrant aroma of femininity to the generation they live
in. The process that began long ago:

The master perfumer had a thought, a design.
He knew it would be special, one of a kind.
The bottle he crafted from his very own hand.
Was ready, now waiting, for the perfect man.
The bottle was like him, no sin, perfectly clean
When to be filled? The perfumer would deem.
The master prepared the fragrance so rare.
With tears on his face he began with care.
The roses were crushed; his tears turned them to liquid.
White jasmine washed clean; revealed the purity within it.
The day had arrived the master knew it would come.
When the fragrance of her would be poured from the Son.
It is then that he lifted the two jars, red and white
And smiled, he knew the result would be delight.
With great care and resolve he began to tip, then pour
Knowing the colors he held meant oh so much more.
The moment was magical, if that is a fair word.
For they say the sound of angels could almost be heard.
As the red and the white came together in the air.
The process that began long ago-Heavenly Pink

The perfect of pinks, from the perfect of loves
Created for her from her father God above.
Man does not make this bottle, this brand;
It reveals our feminine beauty, the mystery of God's
plan.
It serves to remember the grace and the blood
That Christ shed on Calvary, for the Bride that he loves.
So don't leave this wonder on the shelf just to sit.
Wear it, reveal it, draw others to it.
The most beautiful pink shouldn't sit on a shelf.
It should be enjoyed, experienced, yes even felt.
The fragrance of Christ coming out of her skin
The exchange made her righteous, no longer dark sin.
As others draw near, she speaks life all the more,
And tells them about her Lord, the one she adores.

They were both crying. "Olga, what a wonderful story. The wonder of the beauty of Christ and His love for us. The visual picture that rested in the velvet box took my breath away."

Olga smiled a knowing smile, for she had shared this story before.

Timidly, not wanting to break the moment, she said, "May we smell it?"

"Oh, sweet one, you may if you desire . . . however, you are wearing it already." Olga grinned knowingly. "I noticed when you came by at first, and then when I got a little closer I could tell I was right. Your feminine ways are the scent of Christ."

Thrilled, she laughed. "I do? May I buy some of it anyway?"

"No, my dear. This fragrance is not for sale. It must be given."

Olga was already reaching for the drawer. Then she

The Unstoppable Generation

handed her a small, yet identical bottle from inside the box.

"Olga, this cost is too great for you to give it to me."

But Olga smiled and said, "This is what we do. We share our pink and tell our story."

Wanting to show her appreciation, she said, "I'll have to save it for special days so it will last."

Olga broke the seriousness of the moment with a laugh. "Oh dear, that is the other special thing about this perfume. It multiplies, and the bottle—it grows. The more you wear it the more pink will show up. This fragrance increases, it never runs out, it never runs dry.

"Enjoy it every day and all along your way. Others will be drawn to its aroma and you can tell them how it is made: all about Christ, His bride, and their wedding day."

Thank You's were said and hugs exchanged. She left Olga with one last phrase: "You've been so sweet. You smell like Him too."

Walking away, she wiped away a joyful tear from her eye, then gazed down at the bottle looking for the name of the prized perfume. In beautiful letters, words appeared.

"Until He Comes"

NINE

How Big Is Your Brave?

"I am convinced the greatest tragedy is not the sins that we commit but the life that we fail to live. For a lot of us the most spiritual thing we can do is to do something—to turn right when we want to turn left. At worst a passive life is only pitied, yet God counts it as a tragedy when we choose to simply watch life rather than live it."
— Erwin McManus[31]

What if you had the ability to influence the culture? What if you had in you the answer to someone else's question? What roadblocks would you knock down, what obstacles would you go around, to do what you were created to do? Could you be brave?

One woman in the Bible set her mind to accomplish just that, and in one moment in time she changed the course of history.

* * * * *

Yep, little did I know that God would use me to save the nation of Israel. The famous quote from my story is "You were born for such a time as this." I didn't know the great ending of the story as I stood with my hands on the door of the king's throne room. Was I fearless? Yes. But I was also shaking in my royal sandals. People like to quote me with a strong, bold voice declaring: "If I perish, I perish." Truth be told, my voice was quivering and my hands on the door were wet and shaking. What gave me fearless courage? I knew God was really real. I knew, without a doubt, that I could trust him with my life and my people. That fearless courage can be yours as you fight for your family, your nation. And if you are afraid, take my advice—do it anyway. Do it afraid; God really is with you. He knew the timeslot He would place you in and He designed you perfectly for your generation. He has equipped you with a femininity that can be fearless. Do you want it? Daughter of Eve, let me encourage you, stand in your timeslot, be fearless, and press into the destiny of your generation. Be an UnStoppable.

Thinking . . . wearing the crown of courage,
Esther

* * * * *

Whatever you think about the church organization, or the gender debate, God has not called you to sit and discuss. He has called you and His church to go. And bring what is in Heaven to earth. Nowhere in the Scriptures are we called to be relaxed and

UnStoppables laugh at living the little Christian life.

comfortable, waiting for the rapture. UnStoppables laugh at living the little Christian life that only talks or visits with God on Sunday morning rituals. UnStoppables live a big, radical faith every day of every week.

Imagine the impact if every Christian imparted this kind of message to the world they live in on a regular basis. People who would never see the inside of a church would see and experience the love, mercy, and grace coming from the real church.

Living the UnStoppable life is counter-cultural. You will stand out.

Every time you stand up for a good cause, large or small, they'll call you a dreamer, do-gooder, a Jesus freak. Someone will roll their eyes or tell you to sit back down. Keep standing, for in standing your light shines more brightly for more to see. It is about the light, not you, anyway.

Like Linda Smith and her fight to shut down the sex-slave trade. She started an organization called Shared Hope and released "The Protected Innocence Challenge," an in-depth, 207-page report card on the laws in 50 states. Most of the states didn't make the grade. Linda didn't give up; she pressed ahead further and found the state lawmakers very willing to do what was needed to make their states safer. Linda now has gone international to fight trafficking here and abroad.[32]

The Girl Scouts of America has been the focus of recon-struction by the feminist movement since Betty Friedan spent 12 years on the board. This left it a very different institution than the one that had been at the heart of American culture since 1912.

Someone needed to stand up.

Two Texas teens did just that in an era when standing up is hard for adults. Tess and Sydney Volanski did so.

"While we recognized the many good things about Girl Scouts, we had to ask ourselves: Will we stand for our beliefs, for the dignity of life, the sanctity of marriage, modesty, purity? Or will we remain true to Girl Scouts? We cannot see any way to truly do both."[33]

And so they started SpeakNowGirlScouts.com in an effort to expose and remove politics from their beloved organization.

Radical living is what this UnStoppable Generation is called to. And being a radical for Jesus can be risky to your profession. Even famous people, like Kylie Bisutti, can lose when they stand.

Kylie Bisutti beat out 10,000 other contestants in a Victoria's Secret model search. But after two years, she felt convicted, and left the company saying:

"My body should only be for my husband and it's . . . a sacred thing." She reaffirmed her belief that modeling lingerie isn't morally sound. "I didn't really want to be that kind of role model for younger girls," Kylie said.[34]

He brought a radical faith and left a radical church-Don't be a wimpy Christian.

As you can see, anyone, the unknown, the young or the famous, can make a big splash into the sea of sorrow. Standing up for truth, these are the voices of today. What will your voice sound like in the UnStoppable Generation?

"Are the things you are living for worth Christ dying for?"
— Evangelist Leonard Ravenhill's tombstone [35]

Standing Ground

What do you stand for? Instead of finding pretty words and then pretending that's what you stand for, or talking

The Unstoppable Generation

the talk but taking a break the rest of the time, find the ground of your passion and stand on it. You will never rise above what you believe about your God or your life in Him. He brought a radical faith and left a radical church. Don't be a wimpy Christian. Stand! Stand not knowing how it will be done—but stand anyway. Trusting in the God for which we stand. For when we stand for God we are standing on holy ground. Your everyday life can be on God's ground; he makes the path. Get some dirt between your toes and push off. Go.

A Man in Flames

Before Moses led Israel out of Egypt, he had a burning bush moment with God in the desert. God will speak to you anywhere; you only need to be listening. Of course, Moses had a burning bush to help hold his attention. As God spoke to him, the fire on the bush wasn't the only thing that was burning. Moses's heart became ablaze with the holiness of God and the wonder of His request. Moses had all the excuses: too old, too far, not equipped, one guy. And quite frankly, Moses was telling the truth. But God doesn't look at the outside of a man; He sees the heart. Moses possessed a blazing heart of desire to obey, and God would do everything else.

Best of all, God told Moses that He would go with him. Moses agreed, knowing that when the flame is with you, you are UnStoppable.

The Flame and the Spark

Interestingly, the flame of Moses's burning bush and the flame that sets someone to go for Christ comes from the same source: God himself.

In Moses's story, it was not the bush that sustained the flame—it was the flame in the bush. Likewise, for you it is God's flame that burns and sustains passion. It is not of you. Truly, any bush will do. What's got you on fire? Where does your burning desire come from? And what is the source of your flame? Look for the spark, and then wait for His flame. *God* is the passion, not the mission. That is why this chapter will not have a checklist for you. It can only show you what others have done when they went.

So if you feel a spark to be an UnStoppable force for Christ, then go to the flame of God's presence in His Word and in prayer. Like Moses, you will have questions and you will want direction. He doesn't mind questions—he actually likes them because questions form a conversation with Him!

Your motive to live beyond something bigger than you is noble. But it is more important for you to go and serve as your passionate expression of worship to God. Because out of whom you know Him to be does your desire to go come. Then the going becomes about *Him being known by all men*, who in turn worship God.

John Piper puts it best:

> *Missions is not the ultimate goal of the church; worship is. Missions exist because worship doesn't. Worship is ultimate, not missions, because God is ultimate, not man. When this age is over, and the countless millions of the redeemed fall on their faces before the throne of God, missions will be no more. It is a temporary necessity . . . But, worship is also the fuel for missions . . . — Where passion for God is weak, zeal for missions will be weak. Even outsiders feel the disparity between the boldness of our claim upon the nations and the blandness of our engagement with God.*[36]

Small Embers

Not sure where to start? Start at the beginning; that's

what Moses did. Before he went he took off his shoes and got with a holy God and basked in His presence. It is a wise UnStoppable who takes time to get to know the God she gives her life to. After all, you will be trusting him in little and in big ways. You need to know you can rely on Him.

He is faithful and will encourage you and show you His wonder. Read your Bible and books about the character and holiness of God. Your flame for God will soon grow.

Ground Fire

In this generation of social injustice many in our culture will want to rush to the side of the hurting, and many will be effective. However, if they have not taken the God of the flame and the light of the Gospel, they have just temporarily eased the suffering.

Mark 16:15 says, "Go into all the world and preach the Good News to everyone" (NLT). Jesus told his disciples to go into . . . all the world. That means your life—in your world, in your profession. Nowhere did Jesus say, only the missionaries or the pastors or youth groups. There are no professional missionaries, only missionaries that do mission while they do their profession. He said you go, into all the world. It is pretty clear. So live a life on mission and allow the passion in you to direct you to the people you are to share your amazing God and His Gospel with.

Burn Up

Sin and self-doubt. The passion of UnStoppables can easily become a works-oriented passion. So much to do and, with the nature of this breed to be a solver of problems, they can neglect their own problems. It is essential that anyone wanting to live for God understand the trap of legalism and works.

Studying the grace of God and the finished work of

Christ will bring freedom. It will also shut down the enemy as he tries to place self-doubt into the mix. As for sin, that's easy. If you are a believer, all your sins are already paid for. God's not mad at you. He wants you to turn from doing sin and live like He created you to live. Look to Christ for the character, attributes, and ways to walk. And when you see sin in your life, agree with God that it is in fact sin. Repent (which means to agree with God and go His way) and allow the Holy Spirit to strengthen you with grace to do so.

This is how you live a surrendered life that is ablaze for Christ.

Fan the Flame of Faith

When we fan something we believe it will get bigger and burn brighter. Here are some questions to ask yourself. Your answers will help grow the flame of faith. Then believe.

- What are you fanning?
- What problem or cause do you see that needs some of God's light and heat?
- Could this be the moment that your grandchildren will talk about when they tell your story of your life for Christ?

"For we are his workmanship, created in Christ Jesus for good works, which God prepared beforehand, that we should walk in them" (Ephesians 2:10, ESV).

Carry the Flame

Be brave, like Moses, Esther, and the believers who came before you. Don't carry a small light. Take a torch. Be intentional in your passion. Looking for ways to ignite truth and stomp out lies. Show us how big your Brave is.

Don't sit still, move.
Don't fit in, stand out.
Don't sit quietly, speak up[37]
— Seth Godin

Be an arsonist for the Lord. Ignite hearts for the Kingdom. Get in the dirt of life and make something HAPPEN!

TEN

Battle in the Trenches

As an UnStoppable woman, you will need more than a "get it done, head in the clouds" attitude, or even just a good cause to fight for. You will need to get your hands dirty and find some good ground to stand on. Because the enemy of God and our souls desires to kill, steal from, and destroy us. He is not happy about your new fervor, or your desire to please God. His strategy is waged on familiar ground; as with Eve, the soil of our minds provides a great field for battle.

Since the Garden of Eden, Satan has known that women are a powerful influence in the world. That is exactly why he spoke to Eve instead of Adam. For good or bad, life giving or life taking, his goal is to keep her from knowing and executing the fearless femininity that God has designed deep within her.

That is why an UnStoppable She must fortify her life and those she loves with the Word of God and prayer. They are her most powerful weapons against the forces of evil. This issue cannot be taken lightly. As women, we breathe life into the environments we walk in. The feminist movement that believes women can roar has grossly underestimated the power of a woman. This is a good place to note that compassion should be given to the feminists in our midst, for they, our sisters, made in the image of God, have been grossly deceived by the enemy. All of us have been affected in one way or another. Satan has won much in dismantling our gender, families, and culture. However, he is about to take a blow. God is rising up this new breed of believers and the women among them are not going to sit down on the sidelines anymore.

They're a new factor in the equation, a game-changer, and, true to her name she is UnStoppable.

They're a new factor in the equation, a game-changer, and, true to her name, she is UnStoppable. She has drawn a line in the sand and can be heard saying, "Enemy, you're not having our kids anymore, you're not having our families anymore, and you're not having our womanhood anymore." This is the battle cry you will hear from women who stand, with the Word in one hand, her faith in the other, and a fearlessness that comes from knowing who she is and what she can do.

Be the hero for your family and loved ones. It's going to take courage but that is exactly what makes the "she" side of the UnStoppable equation so effective. For if we do not stand in our femininity with fearlessness, there will be a void in the fight. A woman's presences and prayers can make the difference between victory and defeat. Let us not be found prayerless. We must proclaim that we will not stand down, the enemy is not having it his way. Not on our watch!

This book has been all about offering encouragement and warnings to the UnStoppable Generation, those who are called to impact and imprint the world with love, truth, and light. However, there is no amount of cheering or preaching that can instill the power that will be needed to accomplish this movement of God other than the Bible and intimate, relational prayer.

Individually, each of you will need to be faithful in your own quest to know the Word. Fearless in fervent prayer as you walk it out in your daily life. Your own relationship with Christ will overflow, influencing those that come your way with the amazing love of God.

Power From the Spirit

To accomplish productive and deep revelation from time in the Word and prayer, you will need the Holy Spirit's wisdom and help.

As a believer you have the privilege of the Holy Spirit living within you. Now, that may sound a little weird, but that's exactly where God put Him when you received Jesus as your Savior. God sealed all believers with His Holy Spirit for His purpose.

> "And I will ask the Father, and he will give you another advocate to help you and be with you forever—the Spirit of truth. The world cannot accept him, because it neither sees him nor knows him. But you know him, for he lives with you and will be in you" (John 14:16, 17, NIV).

Basically, you carry around with you at all times a counselor, a helper, a teacher, and a guide. It is a mystery that, when realized, brings great joy and peace.

The Inner You

There is a you inside you. It's the one who is thinking and talking in your head. The one who is reading and considering this text. You are not just a mind or a really great body. You are a three-part person who also has a soul.

God created man as spirit, soul, and body.

> *"May God himself, the God of peace, sanctify you through and through. May your whole spirit, soul and body be kept blameless at the coming of our Lord Jesus Christ"* (1 Thessalonians 5:23, NIV).

In short, we are a spirit; we have a soul and we live in a body. Man's spirit is dead until it is born again upon faith in Jesus Christ. It is then that our *spirits* become a new creation, alive because of the salvation offered by Christ Jesus. Our *soul* is our mind, our will, and our emotions. It is our chooser. And our *body* is our physical body, with five senses, blood, and bones.

At salvation the Holy Spirit comes to live in your spirit and you are sealed for eternity on that day. Nothing you do or don't do will ever change the condition of that. He is then your constant companion, providing you with wisdom and grace as your mind is renewed and you walk out the righteousness that is you in Christ.

Inside-Out Living

The Holy Spirit then helps us be conformed into the image of Christ. When changes are made, the light of who Christ is in you shows up on the *outside* of you for the world to see. That is God, glorified through you. Amazing.

The best part is that the Holy Spirit gives you grace to do it all. So what's your part? Listen and obey. Surrender your mind, will, and emotions (soul) to God; believe what He says and your desire to be light will bring light out of you. This is living life from the inside out. This is the UnStoppable lifestyle.

Outside-In Living

In the beginning God created mankind perfectly. The fall that brought death to man physically also brought death to man spiritually. This left every human with the deep knowledge that something was missing. And mankind has been searching to fill that void ever since.

The world that does not know Jesus personally, does not have the option to live from the inside out, for those in the world do not have the Holy Sprit alive in them. And although they were born spirit, soul, and body, their spirits are dead. There is no light in them. They must find answers from earthly avenues. There are many, but the most prominent today, especially with women, is self-actualization.

The age of existentialism has brought about the quest for self-actualization. There are no rules in life other than the ones each individual decides. And there is no universal morality that governs all of us. So to find out what is true for you, the journey of self-actualization is required. It is every man—and woman—for himself, looking for himself.

Their days are filled with self, looking for self, pleasing self, and comforting self. And above all, "bettering themselves."

Truth is no longer absolute, they say. Truth is what is true to you. And only going inward and finding that self can only discover that truth. Unfortunately, all they find there is more of their selves. Their days are filled with self, looking for self, pleasing self, and comforting self. And above all "bettering themselves." They say they are on a journey. That is true, but it is one that has no end. Self-fed, this continual approach will never be satisfied. The result is more of self, pride in finding self, and self-exaltation, because self is supreme.

But as a believer, there was a point when you went from not knowing to *knowing*. You recognized you were not good—in fact, sinful. Accepting the sacrifice of Jesus on the cross as payment for those sins brought new life to your dead spirit. Self died and a new creature was born again in Christ. You, that old self, is gone and the Holy Spirit has taken up residence in you. Your days are filled with your relationship with Him. When comfort is needed you find it in Him; when you are lost, He is your guide; when you are wondering, He testifies to the truth. They say they are on a journey, but you? You have already arrived. The Kingdom of God lives in you and empowers you.

> *When the eyes of the soul looking out meet the eyes of God looking in, Heaven has begun right here on this earth.* — A.W. Tozer[38]

Get a grasp on this, for it is the greatest treasure. Your life in Christ has afforded you more than you could ever imagine. And even if you haven't actually noticed it, He's been there all along, ever since you invited Jesus into your life. You have a personal relationship with the Creator of the universe, the Savior of the world. You have the one that knows everything about everything—like even plumbing!—living in you! This is very good news.

So how can you deepen the relationship with the God of all knowledge and truth? He's got that covered for you too. The Bible is the book that He left for us to read and learn, but also for Him to communicate to us the wonder of who He is and His love for us. So grab a Bible and look at it. The paper is just paper, the ink just ink. But the words are powerful because God inspires them.

How To?

There are many kinds of Bibles and methods of studying. My book, *Table for Two*[39], offers a simple Bible study tool that shows how to do a word search, such as fear vs. faith or jealousy vs. contentment. Just reading the Proverbs will bring wisdom, or reading the Bible in a year—this is another great approach. What method you use isn't as important as how you approach the Word.

Seeing or Seeking the Kingdom

Is this going in one ear and out the other, or are you having an "aha moment"?

It's not the knowledge that we bring into ourselves that counts, but what is brought out of us because we have understood that knowledge. It's what sticks to our hearts that matters.

Knowledge is done with the mind and meditating is done with the heart. Revelation is when both heart and mind understand. Knowledge gained with the mind is that you read it you and understand the concepts of the words and the story. It is an intellectual endeavor and the first step. The second is to meditate on what you read. *Meditation* means to roll over in one's head. It is like marinating meat. The result is still meat, only better, more flavorful and tender.

As we engage our minds during this time, we can come to conclusions that make sense to our human minds and choose to change without ever going into that heart place with God. No one would know, really. The Word is truth and guides anyone who reads it. Believer or nonbeliever, the effects of truth are always good.

However, if we can engage our minds with the truth and then engage our hearts, the Spirit will give us revelation, personal meaning, and understanding. Receiving wisdom from God is like having a train with a car filled with coal; there is always something to keep the train going. But without engaging the Spirit for truth, you are just a really nice train that has no track to take you anywhere.

So develop a teachable spirit in yourself and humble yourself, trusting that a loving God desires a seeking heart and mind. Come before God with a childlike spirit that desires to be taught. Remember, all Scripture will have personal application for those who wait for the revelation from the Holy Spirit. Tuck your morning readings into your heart and asking Him how this applies to you. "Teach me truth." Wait patiently on the Lord. His Word never returns void.

Prayer in the Trenches

The culture is crumbling and the fight is about to get dirty. And being connected to the Lord is going to be essential. Prayer may look like a simple, quiet ordinary activity, but when the God of victory shows up, he will produce the extraordinary.

For instance, the book of Hebrews 11:6 says:

> ...anyone who comes to him must believe that he exists and that he rewards those who earnestly seek him (NIV).

Prayer is the weapon God has given to his children to defeat the devil. While we are given prayer to communicate and receive rest and receive wisdom from the Lord, we are also told to come boldly to the throne of God with our prayers.

The tragedy is not the absence of prayer, but the weak-

The tragedy is not the absence of prayer, but the weakness of it.

ness of it. Jesus told us to pray big prayers, Scripture promise-driven prayers. He gave us authority through His name, His blood, and His Word. The enemy knows the power so he fights in this area to convince us that we are too busy or that we don't know how to pray.

What must that look like in the heavens as man busts through in the spirit realm to pray, calling boldly on the name of the Lord? Can you imagine in your mind's eye, God calling the angels around? "Get ready, guys. This one surely will need Heaven's help. Stand by now, here she comes." The angels and God lean in . . . and all they hear is wimpy whining about pimples and men. To which God replies, "Never mind, guys. A trip to the pharmacy will fix this one." Instead, what if our prayers were prayed with the kind of authority that would not only have angels attentively listening, but their swords pulled and ready to move? As we prayed: "Lord, You said no weapon formed against us would prosper; You said that we are Your children and we have power over the enemy . . . so Lord, I pray that every stronghold that tries to take my children will be defeated. That the carnage of sex trafficking will be defeated and the captives set free. That Your Word would penetrate every school and church in our country for revival to break out in our nation. Lord, that You would empower us to be an UnStoppable force for You, Your love, and Your glory. Amen."

Your powerful prayers honor God. Sometimes He must smile a knowing grin and say, "Hey angels, look at the fearlessness in this little one. She prays like she believes I can actually do that. Go help her."

Girl, the power of Heaven will unleash and start changing when women become this fearless in their prayers. So take a new look at your Bible and your prayer time. Now, just a note to be clear: your soft prayers and tender interchange are always enjoyed by God and should be the bulk of your relationship with him. However, UnStoppable, it is clear— there is a battle and we as women, UnStoppable women are in the trenches fighting for others. Be somebody's hero in prayer today.

Are you Battle Weary?

Many of us are weakened women. Could it be because of the busy pace and stress of our world or the enemy's deception that God doesn't hear prayers? Or maybe it's simply because we don't pray. We unnecessarily live days loaded with the burdens of the world pressing us down, we struggle to stay standing, and we never rest. We are overwhelmed by life— yet relief is but a page away. God's Word. His word and His presence in prayer are quick to administer what we need. Jesus didn't teach His disciples how to do it on their own; He taught them how to pray. Be weak on your knees before God and He will strengthen your stand for when you need to endure in standing. Remember, He is the God who parted the Red Sea and drowned the Egyptian army. Those million Israelites just prayed and they all walked across on dry land. One blast from his mouth can split mountains in two. So get excited to pray; it is quite a daring thing to take God at His Word. Be

To be strong, but you don't have to be as strong as God. He is the ultimate power and He will do it. All glory to Him.

an unstoppable, fearless woman of prayer by putting the forces of darkness on notice.

And remember, you need to be strong, but you don't have to be as strong as God. He is the ultimate power and He will do it. All glory to Him.

ELEVEN

Wild Thoughts on Womanhood

Sometimes the last thing a person wants is advice. Especially a woman. It goes back to that curse-of-Eve thing from Chapter 4. However, in light of the Scripture from Titus, we felt that being honest was better than being silent. Perhaps we could help forewarn and save someone else pain.

> *"These older women must train the younger women to love their husbands and their children"* (Titus 2:4, NLT).

After years of being an UnStoppable, there are a few things we older UnStoppables can bring to the table to offer up as wisdom for you younger ones.

Before we get to the career and callings section, we would like to share some boots-on-the-ground wisdom from our point of view. Some things must be said. We will be honest and vulnerable with you. Bear with us; you are going to like the ending of this chapter. We promise.

Enough Already

For the last 50 years the women's movement hasn't been giving advice, it has been giving orders. And women all over this county have been marching to this drum. But it's been 50 years! And things aren't any better; families aren't better and women aren't happier. Some would say, "Enough already!"

The questions Betty Friedan and her college friends asked in the '60s were actually valid questions. Many of us thought that taking charge was the way to go. It was fun being swept up in something bigger than ourselves. It had the potential to be like a blockbuster movie. The plot was oppression, victims, women as the underdog. The villains were men and there was the hero, in the form of the women's movement. It even had its own music. Sisterhood was at its center and stomping out men was the theme of the era. We had go-go boots because we were going places. We stomped, we roared, we even had our own Virginia Slims cigarettes. We burned our bras and bared our bodies in bikinis. Mini-skirts and hot pants were all the rage. It was sex, drugs, and rock 'n' roll, baby! Nobody was telling us what to do with our bodies or our lives. You get the picture.

But before we romanticize these times, let's be honest about the devastating heartbreak that went with the above list. Most women forgot to factor in the consequences of self-centered demands. The free sex movement that brought about "wife swap" parties and orgies on college campuses. The devaluing of our culture. Stats for STDs, unwanted pregnancies, abortions, and addictions skyrocketed. And the carnage left in marriages from women who needed to "find themselves" pushed divorce rates even higher. Latchkey kids were left alone to care for themselves and daycare became vogue. Interestingly, these issues are not being highlighted as today's media tries to glamorize the era. But we promised to be honest with you, right?

Many feminists now lament the disjointed logic. As feminists, we wanted to be like the men; we wanted to be equal. Huh? We wanted to be the very thing we said we hated! Talk about confusion. Not to mention we were sexually attracted to the men we "hated," but still wanted to marry them, setting up marriages for disaster before we even left the altar. And that doesn't even begin the list of all the other problems, like children, men that won't commit and don't need to, and the big one: lots of regret. In an effort to magnify woman, *woman* was the very one who got lost. For when a woman chooses to be a man, it is a terrible waste of a woman.

> *Huh? We wanted to be the very thing we said we hated. Talk about confusion.*

Girls Gone Wise

Recently, women from this generation have begun speaking up and calling a spade a spade. Mary Kassian, a professor of women's studies and an authority on the women's movement, has boldly led the charge to bring truth to the storyline.

> *Feminism has given us a whole mind-set that personal authority, in particular authority of women, is the most important thing. And instead of bowing to God's authority, we take authority in our own hands*

*and say, "This is the way I want to be. This is the way
I want my world to be. This is the way I want men to
be, and this is the way I want God to be." A physi-
ological quake that shook underground and like a
tsunami, the implications of that have come back
over society in wave after wave . . . the carnage is
unbelievable.*[40]

The feminist defense is always that they achieved much. We now have equal pay for equal work, and we have women CEOs and a woman ran for President. But was this the result of the women's movement or the civil rights movement, which was happening at the same time? All barriers of discrimination were being addressed. What would the results have been? No one knows for sure.

Woman: There's More to You Than You Know

Biblical womanhood's purpose was defined in this book's previous section, on gender. Let's now look at the expression of it. Our bodies are soft and givers of life. It is a high calling to represent this part of God to the world. All women have this honor, but a woman's individual gifts and talents are specific to her. Before time, God planned good works for her to accomplish in the generation in which He would place her.

Did you know that there are many good works? Actually, there are unlimited things you can do. You are not limited to one career or one gift for a lifetime. There is no one job, or one circumstance, or one method. No checklist and no cookie cutter. God has lavished creativity into this creation called woman. He has given each of her a continuous flow of uniqueness. No need to envy another sister in Christ. We were meant to support and nurture each other. To help each other up when we fall, not slam each other down or divide us between methods. As allies against the enemy, our individual strengths make us an unstoppable dynamic force.

Specific and Spacious

Bottom line: we don't need to reinvent ourselves yet again. For when it comes to womanhood, God's design is specific, but the expression of it is gloriously spacious and extremely colorful. Don't allow the world to give you a role. Instead, ask Him. He can do exceedingly, abundantly more than we could ever think or imagine. It's kind of like M&M's. They may come in all colors on the outside, but hidden inside they all have the sweet delight of chocolate waiting for those who will taste and see.

> *God's design is specific, but the expression of it is gloriously spacious and extremely colorful.*

The Mission of Motherhood

There is much advice we could give you reviving our womanhood, but we felt that the greatest destruction of the past decades has been the devaluing of motherhood and children. Next to his own glory, the thing that God values most is human life, people created in His image. He so loves and values people that He gave His life for them so they could be with Him for eternity. Should we value them less?

So, for this book we felt the greatest advice we as older UnStoppables could give you is to value children and the gift of mothering. Not just biological children, but all children. The devaluing and displacing of children is Satan's strategy to destroy the whole of mankind. He desires to destroy all of mankind, so he starts early with the children. If he can get the grown-ups distracted with their own pursuit of things, then he can begin the destruction early. These precious children need heroes in their lives that will keep that from happening. God knew well—he placed children in the arms of mothers and fathers, for protection and love. It is an imperative role. One that will require much knowledge, attention, and diligent prayer.

As women, we must not allow the enemy to distract us by taking the focus off of these precious children that are made in the very image of God himself.

UnStoppable, don't be fooled. Weigh your actions wisely. Who is raising the next generation for God? It is very possible that we could be molding a generation that will usher in the times spoken of in the book of Revelation. Could mothering UnStoppables be one of the purposes God planned for your own life? You may have many careers and many jobs, but they will not compare in relevance to the molding and shaping of children made by God for His glory. It is the greatest honor and the greatest responsibility.

"The generation that is at our knees could be the ones to witness the coming of Christ

"The wise woman builds her house, but with her own hands the foolish one tears hers down" (Proverbs 14:1, NIV).

Here's a sobering thought:
The generation that is at our knees could be the ones

that witness the coming of Christ.

If they are, are they ready? Who has prepared them? The younger children of this generation need the armor and the tools to fight the good fight. They need to be nurtured, taught, and prepared with diligent intention. *UnStoppable: Are you the one your children have been waiting for?*

The Shift

At around the turn of the 20th century, many of us started seeing a shift in the women we were around. We laughingly called it the "that's enough" line. The women who had wanted it all, got it all, and were in charge of it all. Overworked and under-appreciated, many were calling the battle off and hanging up their go-go boots for something more comfortable. Their children grown and their marriages in need of attention, they were turning their focus towards home. One woman said:

> I just got tired of pushing everyone else's paper around. Most of us don't have the glamour jobs we thought we'd have by our age. Crying at my son's graduation, I realized I had missed so much, while other mothers were crying because they hadn't missed a thing. It just wasn't worth it. I went home to be present in the present with my younger children. Mindful of the "now moments," I can push other people's paper in the next decade.[41]

The children of the feminists wanted something for their children that they had not experienced.

Another thing we noticed were the daughters of the

feminist-era women. They were in their early marriage and child-bearing years. Unlike their mothers, who left the home, the move to leave career for a season to take care of their children became a common thread. The children of the feminists wanted something for their children that they had not experienced.

New York Times bestselling author and licensed marriage and family therapist, Dr. Laura Schlessinger, known for her outspokenness, had this to say:

> *Does it seem logical that hands-on, face-to-face interactions during the length of a day between a child and his mother ought to have some kind of profoundly benevolent impact that lasts a lifetime? Or do we really want to believe that human children are no more complex than a goldfish, whose emotional, psychological, and even physical needs might be satisfied with any bowl in any environment as long as there is food to consume? Or is logic not a part of the discussion? Perhaps not.[42]*

Women started to agree with the adage that, "In the eyes of a child a mother can't be duplicated—imitated maybe—but you just can't duplicate her place in the life and day of her child."[43] Books on leaving the workplace and returning to motherhood skyrocketed. Motherhood was in fashion again. Hollywood even began to glorify pregnancy. Unfortunately, abortion and unwed mothers were also increasing. Self was still being defined and valued as supreme, not children or marriage.

Disclaimer: About this spot in this chapter, it gets oooey for readers. Let's make a true statement: this does not apply to all women or all women whose moms worked or to all children of those moms either. It also acknowledges that there are times when a mother or wife must work and daycare is needed. A wife is first a helper to her husband and that can include providing income to support the family. But for now, for this context, it is general, not specific or all-inclusive.

A Very Good Question

So which is it? Where is the answer? My own college-aged daughter approached me with a challenging question.

"Mom, I heard a woman say that she would stay home with her kids, but she'd be bored out of her mind and feel unfulfilled and it would waste her education and career. It seems to me that's a crazy thing to say about your own kids, isn't it?

"But what about the education part? I get that you are into this whole biblical woman stuff and that you value us kids and you think being a professional homemaker is really cool. I know that you want me to feel that way, too. And I do. But why do you and all the women who believe like you push your daughters to go to college? Isn't that a waste?"

I was stunned by her grasp on the last 40 years of female struggle, and her excitement to be a mother one day. I had no answer. I said what every mother would say: "Go to bed. We will talk about it in the morning." Glad for the timeout, I had the night to think about it myself and ask God for wisdom.

The next day, I had it.

The Rectangle

I placed a dollar bill, a check, and her high school diploma on our dinning room table. When she came down that morning, I asked her what they had in common. Her answer was perfect.

"They are all rectangles, mom," she spouted with teen sarcasm.

Pleased at my daughter's sharp thinking so early in the morning, I replied, "Yep. The value of going to college and earning a degree or having children or being a professional homemaker should never be measured by those rectangles. Success, value, or excellence in God's eyes is measured very differently."

Rubbing her eyes and heading for the fridge, she concluded, "Um, so what you're telling me is it's not about the rectangle." We both laughed.

It was a special morning, savoring coffee and sharing truths of womanhood with my daughter. It's no wonder the phrase "It's not about the rectangle" stuck in our family life. It reminds us all that "the rectangle" things made by man do not accurately measure the rewards or successes in life. That it isn't bad or wrong to have or desire those things, in fact, it is good to set goals and see profit from your labors. It is just that not all things should be measured by them.

So What About Education and Motherhood?

As God creates every person, he places deep within them gifts and talents that are uniquely designed for them. Those gifts and talents are entrusted to that person to use however they want. God gives us free choice. If our hearts belong to Jesus, then we want Him to guide the use of those gifts. He gives the gifts, and when we take those gifts and make them the best they can be, it is our gift back to Him.

Going to college helps develops the gifts and talents God has given you. It allows you to be the most excellent you can be for Him. And that is honoring to God.

How About an Example?

Let's say you are gifted in mercy and compassion and

become a nurse. After a few years you are head nurse of your hospital. You get married and start a family and decide to leave your career and become a stay-at-home mom. Have you wasted your education?

No, because choices are not supposed to be primarily made by measuring the rectangle. It's not about rectangles like the dollar bill, or the paycheck, or the diploma. God does not measure things the way we humans do. He measures things by how His precious creation is impacted. God is all about the people, not the rectangles.

So Let's Break It Down

Our nurse in this example has done an excellent job at refining her gift as a nurse. Her gifts of mercy and compassion, along with educational knowledge, landed her a high-paying job at the highest level. God has used her mightily as her excellent gifts and talents blessed many who came to her hospital.

Is it all wasted now that she has chosen to go home and be a mother and professional homemaker? No, it is not wasted. Now that she is a mother, those gifts and talents can be lavished on the most valuable thing God gives to the world: children. She has the honor of bringing life to her children's lives and her home in a way that would not be done if she was absent.

As her children grow and spend time away from her at school, our nurse-mom can volunteer at the hospital or pregnancy center. She might even work at a doctor's office and actually get paid. Getting paid is fine. God isn't against women earning money. Remember, it's not about the rectangle.

It's about the value of people.

Dr. Meg Meeker, bestselling author and physician, has studied families and children for years. Her findings in *10 Habits of Happy Mothers* back up the things so many of us feel.

> *When a mother really understands her value, she has more self-confidence. She sets boundaries with her kids, her husband, and herself, and this makes life more palatable. She is less anxious and feels less inclined to compete with other women, because beneath everything she likes who she is. Finally, mothers who feel valuable can view the larger picture in life, knowing that, while they will always be moms, someday the intense parenting phase will pass and they will be on to utilizing different gifts. We mothers are irreplaceable, and the sooner we avail ourselves of this very simple, deep truth, the more content we can be.*[44]

Educate yourself on the profession of mothering. There are resources in the back that will help you and further encourage you on the mission of mothering.

A Word to Singles

Get excited, girls—the facts are the same for you. Wherever you are in life—single, divorced, or widowed—it's still not about the rectangle. It's about placing value on people above things or money. God's equations are always the same and they always add up to good. As for mothering, it's not only for biological mothers. All women are wired the same, with the nature to nurture, to be life givers to the world. As women, we bring a piece of God's character to every situation and relationship. Singles have the honor to nurture to a broader span of God's children, near home or globally, be it youth groups, nieces and nephews, or spiritual children that you mentor.

Your womanhood was made to bring life into the world. Ask God to show you and be specific with you about the ways your womanhood affects your generation. But, get ready, He just might show you something that will blow your mind.

Seasons

The beauty of God's plan for women is that we have seasons in our lives. The past 50 years of "self-refinement" have removed the enjoyment of the ebbs and flow of life. In their demands of "I want it all, and I can have it all," women forgot one very important thing. God did not intend for us to have it all at one time. He knows us well and what will bring us satisfaction. Instead of rushing to obtain, we should be remaining in the moment we are in. Be a human sponge; soak up every moment and season God gives you. He has so many more, and He longs for you to enjoy the today He has lavishly prepared for you.

God did not intend for us to have it all at one time.

Let's face it, we older UnStoppables were there and involved in the movement, and we are here to tell you the truth. We ended up with it all, plus the responsibility to keep it all. Plus, the awful pressure to make it all work with a smile on our face, because we were supposed to be happy with it all. Ugh—what a circus it was for us! The enemy had lied again. We and our feminist sisters had taken the bait. One feminist-turned-UnStoppable said this with regret about this time in her life:

Nobody's career ever said I love you, Mommy.[45]

The list of quotes available won't fit in this book, but you get the picture. God made woman to receive life into her body and give it out to the world. The bond between

mother and child has always been sacred and mysterious. The last 50 years, Satan has stepped up his plan to
destroy both, with good reason. Even with the rise in abortions and mothers that do not value nurturing and devel-
oping children, this is still the largest generation ever. We
believe he senses the power of this generation of mothers
and their offspring. A woman's touch is one of the most
powerful things on earth. It can be used for good or evil.
This truth is solidified in the William Ross Wallace poem
from 1865 that praises motherhood as the preeminent
force for change in the world.

*The hand that rocks the cradle is the hand that
rules the world.*[46]

We share these things from our hearts as spiritual mothers. For we know the depths of the past pain as we have
had to look at hard truths that have hit square upon
ourselves. We feel the pain of regret as we realized we
missed so much of our womanhood along the way. We
only ask that you seek God for His path for you and seek
His strength to walk it. Search out what God says about
our womanhood, motherhood, and the high value He
places on it.

We have, and though it was a bit embarrassing to ad-
mit some of our miscalculations, God has been faithful to
help us find our mission and our way. And that is why we
challenge you today. Be a hero in the story of womanhood. Be UnStoppable. Our prayers are with you.

TWELVE

Light a Critical Light

Inheritance: *something that is received. It denotes a "putting in the lap of." The receiving generation does nothing good or bad to have an inheritance placed in their laps. –M.C.*

Legacy: *the high privilege of placing an inheritance in the "lap" of the generation that follows. A legacy is the result of a receiving generation taking the inheritance that has been "placed in their own laps" from the previous generation, considering it, and then choosing what they will "place in the lap" of the generation after them. –M.C.*[47]

Getting on the plane headed to Nashville, she was excited to see an aisle seat available. Tired from lectures and worship, she was ready to sit down and stretch out her legs. She found a row that had only a teenager, already asleep with headphones on. She started to take the cherished aisle seat. And this is when an older woman said, "Excuse me, do you mind if I take that aisle seat?" Ugh, she had just been teaching on self-sacrifice and not demanding your own way.

"Sure, I kind of like the middle seat. That way I get to visit with both sides." She smiled, attempting to cheer herself up.

As she settled into the middle seat, her thoughts went to how much she really did like the middle seat. Actually, it was how she had lived most of her life. In the middle.

Discipleship had become her call, leaving a legacy of God's goodness in the laps of the next generation. But she could never have done it alone. Being in the middle also meant that someone who was on the other side of life was placing an inheritance of love and grace and help through the hard times of life back in her direction. She was buckling for takeoff when the older woman pulled a Bible out of her purse and said, "Thank you for the seat. Do you know Jesus?"

She could almost feel God smiling as she realized the middle seat really is a great place to travel.

The Cry of a Generation

"Will you disciple me?"

"I can't read my Bible. Will you meet with me for coffee and show me how?"

"I really could use some advice on how to have a prayer time. What do you do?"

There is a cry in this generation of women. A cry for connection with God and other women. They need help with their marriages, dreams, and hang-ups, and so they stand in the Christian bookstore looking for something that will give them some encouragement. They are longing for the arms of a real live woman who has been there and done that. One who will tell her it's going to be OK and to help her pray. They grew up learning from *Sesame Street* and other technology-saturated entertainment. Their church Bible studies have women, but the format is teaching with—of all things—a video on the television. They sigh, thinking, *This just must be how life is.* They are wondering where all the women aged 40s and up went. With our mobile society, so many women are miles away from their grandmas and aunties.

Well, I am here to tell you this is NOT the way it is supposed to be. And whether you are looking up in age for a mentor or peering over your shoulder to disciple, God is watching us all, urging us to engage. Those of us who are engaged continue to be booked solid and are thin on time. We too wonder if reinforcements are coming. We feel like Joshua and Caleb standing at the Jordan River with a million wilderness kids who had never seen a battle. But we aren't worried; we know how that story ended. Joshua and Caleb had the adventure of their lives and God enabled the Israelites to conqueror the Promised Land. They all lived out their lives together, relishing the glory of their awesome God.

Where did this massive void in our Christian culture come from? No one really knows for sure. Was it, as Jim Hybels and other leaders concluded a few years ago, the mistake that was made when the church began focusing on "seeker-friendly" programs and services? Leaders now realizing they had neglected discipleship and teaching believers how to mature? Or was it older believers who were off living their own lives, still caught in the self-actualization mode, disconnected from those that needed their wise advice?[48]

Abandoned might be too strong of a word, but what they are looking for are those who seek someone to come alongside them and do life. It has left them feeling more like orphans rather than connected children within the family of God. Whatever the cause, it is now very clear that the church is in dire need of men and women who will help launch the next generation into its promised land.

Blame

Bible literacy in the body of Christ is at an all-time low. For too long we have expected the church and its leaders to fill all the roles need for the members to grow up. Friend, it isn't a small group of people standing at the river's edge of tomorrow's promised land. It is an army of UnStoppables, and there are plenty of places for you to put your feet. Step out of your comfort zone and join the strong and courageous Joshuas and Calebs of today.

Step out of your comfort zone and join the Joshua and Calebs of today.

The new breed of UnStoppables is pressing the older believers to engage. Searching out wisdom, this breed is on a mission and their fire has them blazing. The UnStoppables live forward-focused, full of a fresh determination that is always moving ahead. Not focused on the past, but forward toward solutions. But all that moving forward and not learning from the past can invite mistakes that cause them to stumble, and cause victories to be lost. They will go on without the older era of their generation if need be; they have their God and He will provide.

God Created Family

We laugh when one of our children is given a family tree assignment for school. It has more branches that run together . . . it looks more like a vine than a tree. We just keep adding; there's always room for one more.

God knows the value of family working together. He designed it in society and in the church. He has heard the cries of His children and He is assembling believers from this generation, younger and older, "hes" and "shes" of every race, color, and creed. Uniquely wiring them to move in this time, for Him, in a powerful way. Some believe this is the reason for the longing for connection and community. It is a drawing of the UnStoppables.

When societal culture begins talking of generational, racial, and economical gaps, UnStoppables don't get offended because they know something the media and the world doesn't know. Instead of getting angry, these forward-movers just move on, laughing. They recognize the devil's "division" games. He seeks to "divide" the "vision" and destroy. Division and destruction is one thing UnStoppables are very familiar with. They have felt the pain and seen the wreckage division causes, in marriages and families all across this country. And they are intent to keep the enemy from playing those games with them. This may be one of the reasons for the strong desire for someone to come alongside. They long to know how to do battle, read their Bibles for truth, and how to pray powerful, unstoppable prayers.

What Gap?

They are not fooled by negative generation-gap rhetoric, for they have seen the powerful effect when eras overlap. They lovingly call it the "generational sweet spot." It is the place where discipleship, mentoring, connection, and community happen. There, the steel-gray strength of truth and the tender unconditional love of grace mesh to create a very soft place to land for both youth and elders. Indeed, a sweet spot to be celebrated.

And in a world that can be sharp and pressing, it is a rare, precious place indeed. It is a place where the idealism and enthusiasm quality of youth overlaps with the wisdom and experientially confident quality of the mature. Both eras find that the other infuses them. Together they are propelled to move forward. Their fuel is the Word of God, the method is following in the footsteps of Jesus. And just like the disciples from the book of Acts, they are moving forward, fully expecting to turn the world upside down.

Welcome

This special, generational sweet spot is the place where discipleship takes place, fellowship is to be had, and community grows healthy. It is a place of intentional engagement, where receiving an inheritance and leaving a legacy are joyously exchanged.

It is the middle seat. Do you have one?

Discipleship Defined

In the secular world *mentoring* is a common phrase. Discipleship is a lot like that. Take the example of insurance sales. A new sales guy is told it is a very good idea to find a seasoned sales rep to learn the ropes from. He wants to be a success, to follow in the footsteps of someone who accomplished what he wants to accomplish. The two meet, the older one gives advice, and the younger one—who is so excited about his new job—receives the help. Both leave energized.

Discipleship is a lot like that. It is a term that is most commonly used in the Christian world. Following the example of Jesus as He discipled the Twelve. Those twelve desired to learn what Jesus knew about spiritual things. Jesus was also their mentor as He mentored them in life skills and practical application. Both words, discipleship and mentoring are used in the Christian culture.

Basically, spiritual discipling takes place when a believer of any age meets with another believer who has been where they are, relationally or spiritually. Only, instead of *showing* them the ropes, like in the secular world, the mentor is *holding* the ropes. She or he is offering the way to Bible study, encouragement, and compassion. It is the true discipler, The Holy Spirit, that is the ultimate counselor, teacher and guide. The mentor/discipler is the physical arms and warm smile. What takes place between the mentor, the person being discipled and the Holy Spirit is life changing. A sweet spot, indeed.

Its about teaching and directing another to be God dependent.

How?

In my book *Table for Two: Doing Life and Savoring the Scriptures Together*, my co-author, Amy Pierson, and I make it very easy for you to start a mentoring/discipleship relationship. Here are a few suggestions from the book.[49]

Looking for Someone to Disciple?

Start by praying and asking God to show you someone with whom you might have something in common. Not someone to have coffee with once a week. Iron sharpens iron, so ask yourself if you are ready to be the iron for someone else.

It is recommended that it be same-sex grouping. Unless, that is, it is within a family, which is where discipleship is supposed to be taking place every day.

Due to the fall of the family, there are multitudes of people who desire for someone to come along and show them the Word, how to study the Bible, how to pray, and more. You may find that others start flocking to your sweet overlap spot. But don't overload yourself. Make a waiting list and pray for more women to help.

Looking For a Mentor

You could find her anywhere. Pray and ask God for the right someone to help you grow in your faith. A good candidate would be someone who intentionally engages in relationships for Christ. Her core strength is her relationship with God, fueled by prayer. The motive is to imprint the lives of those she sits with for

How did Jesus mentor his disciples? He told them stories, and those stories are left for you to tell too.

the Kingdom of God. She is always at the ready. She is trustworthy and transparent. Truth is on her tongue, and when you have left her, the residue of God's Word is what you remember.

For more resources on how to disciple, check the resources in the back of the book for help. Another source for information is www.amazingthings.com. This is my ministry website, and there you will find material, support, and discipleship for yourself.

Why?

Matthew 28:19 and 20 tells us:

"Therefore go and make disciples of all nations, baptizing them in the name of the Father and of the Son and of the Holy Spirit, and teaching them to obey everything I have commanded you. And surely I am with you always, to the very end of the age" (NIV).

Go and make disciples. It was clear to them what He meant because they themselves had been discipled by the greatest disciple-maker, Jesus. How did Jesus mentor His disciples? He told them stories, and those stories are left for you to tell too. Get your Bible and read those treasured words together. Then, together, discuss them, looking for God's character in the stories. Jesus told them to watch Him, because He would do what His Father did. Jesus was a disciple. He watched His Father in Heaven and did what He did. It is important that if you are mentoring someone that you be looking to Jesus.

Discipline without biblical discipleship leaves a child untrained in the truth of God.

There is a three-minute, power-packed Youtube video that provides a great explanation of being a maker of disciples. Christine Cain inspires us all to drop the nets of our daily lives and make disciples for Christ. It can be found at: http://www.youtube.com/watch?v=hnIiGeX-MukI[50] (Or simply search for Christine Cain's "Fishers of Men" clip at YouTube.com.)

Family Discipleship

Start at home with your own loved ones. This was God's original plan. To have mothers and fathers teach their children about Him. Don't think you have to know it all. Many of us have no idea how to lead or teach another person—even our children—how to follow Christ. We assume that once they are saved, we are done. Nothing could be further from the truth. God's man-on-display plan of showing Himself to the world is with us until our last breath. We seem to understand that we need to train our children and discipline them when they do wrong. However, it is very important to understand that:

Discipline without biblical discipleship leaves a child untrained in the truth of God.

According to the Barna Research Group, being discipled within ones family is one of the foundational things that keep young adults close to God after they leave high school. They will look to someone to show them the way. Let that someone be you.

Just start. If you get a question you can't answer, then show your daughter what it looks like for you to be discipled. Go and find the answers together. The bond of seeking God together is a powerful picture of the church working together in that generational sweet spot.

Keep It Simple

Because of my discipleship ministry, I get a lot of questions about what I do and what discipleship is. I say it's simple. It's all about pointing. I am a pointer. Pointing to Jesus. Pointing to Scripture. Pointing to areas of life that someone is struggling in and pointing to answers. Pointing to my own life stories and pitfalls. It is not about being a counselor and it is not about being co-dependent. It is being a listener, compassionate, empathic, and yes, pointing.

Sometimes I feel like an air traffic controller bringing in a plane for landing hoping it doesn't crash. It is about teaching and directing another to be God-dependent.

It's being a welcoming hug and a soft place to land for a good cry. It is simple, but it is the most rewarding thing a woman can do. Being a pointer and fulfilling the unique design of a woman to be a helper and life giver to all who come will bring you great joy and fulfillment.

The "Someday" Trap

Because it is so personal, people tend to put off this high calling of discipling. They fall into one of two categories: The "I don't know enough about the Bible" trap or the "manana" trap. Manana actually means "not today" in Spanish. That mentality never produces. I find that both, often, can be used as excuses. No one knows everything about the Bible. But you know life, you know what it feels like to be confused, or hurt, or thrilled and excited. The Holy Spirit will be your guide. With him, your life experience, the Bible, a good book, and an honest approach—all these things will soon have you on your way.

The truth may be that you just might not be like Joshua and Caleb. The ones who said God is faithful. Their attitude was: "If he said we are supposed to do this, we will." You might not want to be a part of the UnStoppable Generation. But chances are, if you are in the last chapter of this book, God just might be calling you to the generational sweet spot of discipleship.

Strike a Match

Take courage. You bear God's whisper within. You are imprinted with His identity and power-packed with His love. You are well equipped to influence a generation that hungers for the real, live arms of spiritual mothers who have been there and done that. And when you do, your voice breathes life and your hands pass the warmth of God's love.

Never underestimate the power of just being in someone's life. Imagine what would happen if your knowledge of the radical, unconditional grace of Christ was intentionally ignited in a generation. It would light a flame. That flame would light the path to go share it with another, and so on and so on, until an entire generation would bear the light of the Gospel. They would be UnStoppable.

Take courage. You bear God's whisper within.

Be fearless, light a critical light for the generation that longs to see you be brave, a generation that longs to be brave too. All of Heaven and earth are waiting for the ones who will show themselves as fearless for the glory of God. For within the record of time, they will forever be known as The UnStoppable Generation.

▶▷▶EPILOGUE◀◁◀

Drama: An Inheritance Received and a Legacy to Give

Entering the house, she dropped her things on the entry hall table and sat on the steps. Rubbing her eyes, she started to recall the roller coaster of emotions. Grams's funeral and all the tears it brought, and receiving that mysterious Inheritance Box. And what about all the amazing discoveries about biblical womanhood? The laughter at the mall with her best friend lightened things up. Olga and the inspiring bottle of pink perfume could easily have been the best surprise of all. She felt as if her whole world had been picked up like a snow globe and been given a big shake.

It now appeared that the seemingly calm life she had been living was upside down—according to God's directions. A sense of release and peace hit her soul. It was all right. Her life had been turned right side up. She had a purpose and God had a plan. It was true; she was an UnStoppable in a crazy world. And her life would never be the same.

Confidence rose in her and she said out loud: "But it's my world, and I have been called to such a time as this, crazy though it may be. I was perfectly designed for it." And a giggle slipped out as she stood up on the stairs.

She glanced at her things on the entry room table. Her

mind went to the bottle of pink perfume. She tentatively reached into her bag as if she wasn't sure if it had been a dream or if the bottle was truly there. She felt the cool glass; it was. With a smile she pulled the beautiful crystal bottle out. It was even more beautiful than she had remembered though all of that was just hours ago.

Gazing deep into the pink liquid, she remembered anew that she was made for more than big houses, hip clothes, or . . . God had uniquely designed her as a woman to live exactly where she was, for a bigger purpose than herself.

She was to display His glory in her world, through her womanhood.

With her newfound knowledge of God's Word and a real grasp on the crazy world she lived in, she knew the Lord would show her how and where to shine His light and how to draw her generation into the truth.

It would be counter to the ways of the culture. But the culture wasn't the goal. Living for Christ as a woman in a way that reflects God for his glory—this was the goal. Bold, yet soft. Fearless, yet fragrant. She would stand by her sisters and brothers in Christ and go out to impact every corner of their world. For they are the generation called . . . UnStoppable.

She felt her inner core strengthen as she lifted her head. Courage is the only way to describe what she felt. Her mind was racing as she remembered the worship and the Word of God that she had taken into herself. She was lost in the glory of it all.

And this is when a cherished voice from the kitchen aroused her from her thoughts . . .

"Mom . . . I'm home from practice. Hey, what's this big trunk? It says 'Inheritance'? And what's the deal with this apple? It stinks."

Smiling, she turned and headed toward her daughter, her legacy. Then she paused and reached back for the pink-filled crystal bottle. For there, in her own world, was another little one just waiting to be . . . an UnStoppable She.

RECOMMENDED READING

-*The Feminist Mistake, The Radical Impact of Feminism on the Church and Culture*, Mary Kassian, Crossway, Wheaton, IL

-*Girls Gone Wise*, Mary Kassian, Moody Publishing, Chicago, IL

-*Radical Womanhood: Feminine Faith in a Feminist World*, Carolyn McCulley, Moody Publishing, Chicago, IL

-*True Woman 101*, Nancy Lee DeMoss and Mary Kassian, Moody Publishing, Chicago, IL

-*In Praise of Stay at Home Moms*, Dr. Laura Schlessinger, HarperCollins, New York, NY

-*The Mission of Motherhood*, Sally Clarkson, Waterbrook Press, Colorado, CO

-*The New Eve*, Robert Lewis, B&H Publishing, Nashville, TN

-*Lioness Arising*, Lisa Bevere, Waterbook Press, Colorado Springs, CO

-*The Next Christians: How a New Generation is Restoring Faith*,Gabe Lyons, Double Day, NY

-*The Organic Church: Growing Faith Where Life Happens*, Neil Cole

-*Red Moon Rising*, Pete Greig & Dave Roberts, Relevant Books, Winter Park, FL

-*Revolution: Worn Out on Church?*, George Barna, Tyndale House, Carol Stream, IL

-*Chasing Daylight*, Erwin Rahael McManus, Thomas Nelson, Nashville, TN

-*The Absolutes*, James Robison, Tyndale House Publishers, Inc.

-*The Pursuit of God*, A.W. Tozer, Wing Spread Publishers, Camp Hill, PA

-*Humility*, CJ Mahaney, Multnomah Books

-*I Am Not But I Know I AM*, Louie Giglio, Multnomah Books

-*Supernatural Skyline*, Jim Hylton, Destiny Publishers, Shippensburg, PA

-*Pure Grace, Clark Whitten*, Destiny Image Publishing, Shippensburg, PA

-*Table for Two: Doing Life and Savoring the Scriptures Together*, Mona Corwin and Amy Peirson, LifeWay, Nashville, TN

-*Women Counseling Women*, Elyse Fitzpatrick, Harvest House, Eugene, Oregon

-*The Origin of the Bible*, Phillip W. Comfort, Tyndale House Publishers, Inc.

-*I Don't Have Enough Faith to Be an Atheist*, Norman Geisler, Crossway, IL

NOTES

Chapter 1

1.Jim Hylton, *The Supernatural Skyline, Where Heaven Touches Earth* (Shippensburg, PA: Destiny Image Publishers, Inc.), p. 47.

2.a. Leeland, *Awaken, The Great Awakening CD*, Provident Label Group LLC, September 20, 2011, used by permission.

2.b. Toby Mac, *Unstoppable, Eye On It* CD, Achtober Songs Publisher, 2012, used by permission

3. A.W. Tozer, *The Pursuit of God* (Camp Hill, Pennsylvania: Wing Spread Publishers), p. 1.

4. Ed Stetzer, part of the research department of LifeWay in Nashville, shared in a message given at Northwood Church, Keller, Texas, November 1, 2009.

5. Claude Hickman, *Live Life On Purpose* (Enumclaw, WA: Winepress Publishing),
p. 27.

Chapter 2

6. Gallup research, website, Religion, http://www.gallup.com/poll/1690/religion.aspx.

7. Barna Group website article: "A Faith Revolution Is Redefining the Church," Oct 10, 2005, www.barna.org/barna-update/5-barna-update/170-a-faith-revolution-is-redefining.

8. Barna Group website article: "Three Spiritual Journeys of Millennials," May 9, 2013, www.barna.org/barna-update/millennials/612-three-spiritual-journeys-of-millennials.

Chapter 3

9. Hickman, p. 19.
10. Pete Greig & Dave Roberts, *The Vision Poem, Red Moon Rising* (Winter Park, FL: Relevant Books) selected sections used.
11. 24/7 Website, www.24-7prayer.com/about/story.
12. Trek-X website, www.mobilizingstudents.com.
13. Interview with Chris White, August 12, 2013.
14. Church of the City website, www.churchofthecity.com.
15. *The Blaze*, article, Jan 2, 2013, www.theblaze.com/stories/2013/01/02/jesus-generation-60000-students.
16. *The Christian Post*, July 23, 2013, www.christianpost.com/news/hillsong-united-welcome-zion-tour.

Chapter 4

17. Gabe Lyons, *The Next Christians* (New York: Doubleday), p. 73.
18. N. T. Wright, *Simply Christian* (HarperCollins Publisher), p. 123.

Chapter 5

19. S.E. Cupp, *Carolina Journal* news report. "Has Feminism outlived its Usefulness?" June 3, 2011.
20. Karen Salmansohn, *Oprah Magazine*, November 5, 2009, www.oprah.com/spirit/Are-You-a-Feminist.

Chapter 6

21. The Free Dictionary By Farlex, www.thefreedictionary.com.
22. Ibid.
23. Ibid.
24. Original poem, by Mona Corwin, 2012.

Chapter 7

25. J. Steve Lee, apologetics pamphlet, 2009.

26. Rick Renner, *Sparkling Gems in Greek* (Tulsa, OK: Teach All Nations), p. 856.
27. John Piper, True Woman Conference, 2008.

Chapter 8
28. Nancy Leigh DeMoss, *Voices of the True Woman Movement: A Call to the Counter-Revolution* (Chicago: Moody Publishers); also found at www.womenshistory. about.com/od/quotes/a/de_beauvoir_2.htm.
29. Toby Mac, *Speak Life, Eye On It* CD, Label ForeFront, Producer, TobyMac 2012, by permission.
30. Original poem, by Mona Corwin, "Good-bye," 2011.

Chapter 9
31. Erwin McManus, *Chasing Daylight* (Nashville, TN: Thomas Nelson), pp. 36, 45, 46.
32. Matt Kaufman, "Stopping Traffic," *Citizen* Magazine, March 2012.
33. Bob DeMoss, "Answering the Call," *Citizen* Magazine, August 2011.
34. www.nypost.com/2013/04/24/i-gave-up-modeling-for-god, April 24, 2013.
35. en.wikipedia.org/wiki/Leonard_Ravenhill; a photo can be found at this site, also.
36. John Piper, *Let the Nations Be Glad* (Grand Rapids, MI: Baker Publishing), pp.15, 36.
37. Seth Godin, blog: "This or That?", August 3, 2012.

Chapter 10
38. A.W. Tozer, *The Pursuit of God* (Camp Hill, PA: Wing Spread Publishers), p. 86.
39. Mona Corwin and Amy Pierson, *Table for Two: Doing Life and Savoring the Scriptures Together* (Nashville, TN: LifeWay Publishers).

Chapter 11

40. Mary Kassian, True Woman Conference lectures, and "Feminism and the Christian Woman" promo clip, Indianapolis, Indiana, 2010.
41. Anonymous.
42. Dr. Laura Schlessinger, *In Praise of Stay-at-Home Moms* (New York: HarperCollins), pp. 17,18.
43. Mona Corwin.
44. Dr. Meg Meeker, *The 10 Habits of Happy Mothers: Reclaiming Our Passion, Purpose and Sanity* (New York: Ballantine Books), p. 15.
45. Schlessinger, p. 76.
46. William Ross Wallace, "The Hand that Rocks the Cradle," poem. It can be found at www.en.wikipedia.org.

Chapter 12

47. Mona Corwin. Paraphrased for ease of understanding from Greek definitions; referenced from www.biblestudytools.coms/lexicons/greek.
48. Bob Burney, Baptist Press, Nov. 6, 2007, wwww.bpnews.net/bpnews.asp?Id=2678.
49. Corwin and Peirson.
50. Christine Cain, Catalyst Conference. Atlanta, "Fishers of Men" Clip, Oct. 10, 2012, www.youtube.com/watch?v=hnliGeXMukl.